Tools for Writing

Linda Robinson Fellag
Community College of Philadelphia

Laura Tomassi Le Dréan
University of Houston-Downtown

Heinle & Heinle Publishers

ITP An International Thomson Publishing Company

Pacific Grove · Albany · Bonn · Boston · Cincinnati · Detroit · London · Madrid · Melbourne · Mexico City
New York · Paris · San Francisco · Singapore · Tokyo · Toronto · Washington

The publication of *Tools for Writing* was directed by the members of the Newbury House Publishing Team at Heinle & Heinle:

Erik Gundersen, **Editorial Director**
John F. McHugh, **Market Development Director**
Kristin Thalheimer, **Production Services Coordinator**

Also participating in the publication of this program were:

Publisher: Stanley J. Galek
Editorial Production Manager: Elizabeth Holthaus
Project Manager: Rachel Youngman, Hockett Editorial Service
Assistant Editor: Karen P. Hazar
Production Assistant: Maryellen Eschmann
Manufacturing Coordinator: Mary Beth Hennebury
Photo Researcher: Denise Theodores
Interior Designer: Winston · Ford Visual Communications
Illustrator: Brian Orr
Cover Artist: William Waitzman

Heinle & Heinle Publishers
20 Park Plaza
Boston, MA 02116 USA

International Thomson Publishing
Berkshire House 168-173
High Holborn
London WC1V 7AA
England

Thomas Nelson Australia
102 Dodds Street
South Melbourne, 3205
Victoria, Australia

Nelson Canada
1120 Birchmount Road
Scarborough, Ontario
Canada M1K 5G1

International Thomson Publishing Gmbh
Konigwinterer Strasse 418
53227 Bonn
Germany

International Thomson Publishing Asia
221 Henderson Road #05-10
Henderson Building
Singapore 0315

International Thomson Publishing - Japan
Hirakawacho-cho Kyowa Building, 3F
2-2-1 Hirakawacho-cho
Chiyoda-ku, 102 Tokyo
Japan

2 3 4 5 6 7 8 9 10 XXX 01 00 99 97 96 95

Library of Congress Cataloging-in-Publication Data

Fellag, Linda Robinson.
    Tools for writing / Linda Robinson Fellag, Laura Tomassi Le Dréan.
        p.   cm.
    ISBN 0-8384-5294-9
    1. English language—Textbooks for foreign speakers.   English
language—Composition and exercises.   I. Le Dréan, Laura Tomassi.
    II. Title.
PE1128.F4245   1994
    428.2'4—dc20   94-28720
                                                                CIP

Contents

Chapter 2   Stories We Tell 23

Chapter 9   The Order of Things 173

Preface

This intermediate- to high-intermediate level textbook presents an effective classroom approach to both the student's writing *process* and to his or her final *product*. Using a purely process-oriented paradigm for teaching writing has not always proven successful, as our experience with process-driven textbooks has shown. Even process advocates (Raimes 1985; Zamel 1987) have acknowledged that teachers need to attend to *product* as well as *process* in teaching second-language (L2) writing. With these needs in mind, we have developed *Tools for Writing* to allow students not only to experience the writing process but also to utilize "instructional scaffolding" (Langer and Applebee 1986) or "tools for writing" that will help them create more viable products.

L2 writing students are often unable to shoulder the burden of providing content, organization, and a certain level of linguistic fluency. Especially at the intermediate level, L2 writing students face critical challenges. On the grammatical level, writers are expected to exhibit control over structures they have already "learned," while being exposed to increasingly complex patterns. Rhetorically, writers "in the middle" are asked to produce an array of different modes of academic writing, often with little direction from textbooks. Finally, lexically, writers are challenged to acquire an increasing stock of vocabulary but are rarely aided in using vocabulary for particular writing tasks.

ESL teachers must design writing tasks carefully to meet *all* the L2 learners' needs. Our criteria in creating the writing assignments in *Tools for Writing* include the following:

- The writing atmosphere must be stimulating and supportive.
- Writing tasks must be communicative and engaging.
- Writers should collaborate, when feasible, to gather ideas.
- Grammatical application and control must be facilitated.
- Vocabulary generation and expansion must be encouraged.
- Organization of content into academic writing style must be explicitly presented and practiced.
- Revision and editing must be stressed as part of the writing process.
- Writers should use journals to express themselves freely.

Applying what researchers term a "structured process approach" to teaching writing, we have designed this textbook to help intermediate students gain the skills necessary to discover, organize, and develop topics. Innovative activities in each chapter are thematically based to suggest content and organization, and thus, to free students to concentrate on expression. But the schemata are far removed from the traditional method of assigning topics and prescribing rhetorical models. We integrate process activities—brainstorming, freewriting, peer review—and stress audience and purpose. In each chapter, students get ideas from films, music, readings, group projects, and each other; they also generate appropriate vocabulary, practice relevant grammatical structures, and discover possible rhetorical paths for their content.

After five years of testing this approach in an intensive, preacademic English context, we have found it successful in guiding L2 writers to explore ideas. At the same time, this approach helps them develop fluency and focus in their writing.

Organization

Each chapter of *Tools for Writing* is organized thematically. Chapters also progress in order of rhetorical, linguistic, and thematic difficulty, moving generally from personal to public topics, and from paragraph- to essay-length compositions. Less complex rhetorical patterns—narration and description—precede more complicated organizational patterns: exposition, process, cause/effect, comparison/contrast, and classification.

Description

Each chapter consists of the following sections:

Getting Ideas

This section consists of readings, photographs, drawings, questionnaries, audio-video sources, and other stimuli for writing. The idea-gathering process also includes engaging class and group activities, such as paired observations, interviewing, freewriting, and brainstorming, in which students collaborate to generate ideas.

Composing

This section includes tasks to help writers organize, develop, and unify their writing into acceptable rhetorical forms. These tasks teach students about topic sentences, support, coherence, unity, audience, purpose, essay organization, thesis statement, introductions, conclusions, body paragraphs, transitions, outlining, and organizational options.

Building Language Skills

Grammatical and lexical work in each chapter exposes the writers to structures and vocabulary items most likely to be applied to particular writing tasks. The emphasis in this section is on deductive recognition and practice rather than on presentation of structures.

Writing

Each chapter except chapter 1 presents two complete writing modules—two sets of tasks designed to provide students with the "tools" they need to accomplish two writing assignments. The writing assignments have been selected to facilitate language learning as well as to promote the students' interest in written communication. Tasks within each assignment may be omitted, depending on a particular class's needs. In addition, more writing topics are presented at the close of each chapter.

Revising

Students engage in peer revision and editing of all compositions, focusing first on global content and organization problems and then on specific grammatical and lexical errors in writing. Self-revision and editing are also facilitated.

Journal Writing

Controlled and free-topic journal assignments are a focal point of each chapter, enabling students to reflect on writing and other concerns.

More Writing Topics

Additional writing topics at the end of each chapter give students further opportunities to explore the chapter themes.

Questions and Comments

If you have questions about the materials or, after using them, have feedback that you are willing to pass along to us, we would be happy to hear from you via Heinle & Heinle.

Acknowledgments

The authors wish to thank all the students of the English Language Institute at the University of Houston-Downtown who contributed their writing to this textbook. Additionally, we would like to acknowledge Gail Kellersberger, director of the English Language Institute, for her encouragement and support. At Heinle & Heinle Publishers, we wish to thank ESL assistant editor Karen Hazar for her guidance, and our reviewers, Teresa D. O'Donnell, Northern Virginia Community College; Lois I. Wilson, University of Pittsburgh; and Caroline Schwarzwalder, North Shore Community College, for their input in developing this book.

Chapter 1

The Classroom Community

Who do you write for—yourself or others?

Do you learn anything about yourself when you write?

What do you think you can learn from your classmates' writing?

Welcome to your writing community!

Look around. You may see faces of students whose countries you do not know about. You may wonder whether you have anything in common with the people next to you, besides learning a new language. This "global community" may seem strange, but it can be enriching. That is because you can accomplish another goal as you improve your English: You can gain an understanding of the world through your classroom community.

Begin by thinking of yourselves as a community of writers. Be prepared to draw from your intellectual, personal, and cultural differences. And don't be surprised if you find you share many of the same opinions, dreams, stories, and problems.

As you collaborate in writing, you can discover yourself and others, and you can express yourself more confidently and clearly in English. Through the tools in this textbook, you can also learn to organize your ideas, enhance your vocabulary, and refine your grammatical control.

To initiate this community effort, begin by learning more about your class. In this activity, you will tell each other about yourselves.

WRITING ASSIGNMENT 1

A Paragraph for the Class

Getting Ideas

PERSONAL T-SHIRTS

To make a personal T-shirt follow these steps:

1. On a piece of paper, 11 inches by 17 inches or larger, draw a T-shirt large enough to write on. Use a marker in a favorite color.

2. Follow your instructor as he or she draws a personal T-shirt on the chalkboard, putting this information on the shirt:
   - In the center of the shirt, write the name you wish to be called in this class.
   - Under your name, draw a picture or write a word to represent your favorite pastime.
   - On the neck of the T-shirt, write a word that describes how you want other people to view you. (Use an adjective like *honest, kind,* or *funny.*)
   - On the right-hand sleeve of the shirt, write the name of an important person or of a loved one. If you write a loved one's name, draw a heart if you wish.
   - On the left-hand sleeve of the shirt, write or draw two things that you do well.
   - On the bottom, left-hand corner of the shirt, write one bad quality or bad habit you want to change about yourself.
   - On the bottom, right-hand corner of the shirt, write a word or two about a dream you have for your future.

3. Next, in a small group, hold up your paper T-shirt and tell your group about yourself. Do this by explaining the information you have written on your T-shirt. Your instructor will model this activity by telling the class about his or her own T-shirt.

4. When everyone in your group has finished presenting the shirts, exchange T-shirt papers. On the back of the shirt of each of your group members, write one question about something that appears on the front of the shirt. Ask a question to get more information about something on the shirt.

5. After everyone has written a question on each other's papers, take your T-shirt back. Taking turns, answer the questions on the back. If someone has written you a question that you do not wish to answer, simply say "Pass."

6. At the end of your discussion, give your T-shirts to your instructor.

Writing

WRITING ABOUT YOURSELF

To introduce yourself and your writing to your instructor, look over your T-shirt and choose one item on the shirt as a subject for a short composition about yourself. Write only about one thing on your shirt. For example, if you wrote *drawing* as one of your talents, you may want to write about that.

After you write, post your T-shirt on a classroom wall.

Composing

CLASS AUDIENCE

In writing, the audience means the people you write to and for. Knowing the background and interests of your audience helps you to choose what to write about, and helps you to direct how you write for that special group.

For example, if one of your pastimes is mahjong, and if you wish to write about this, you might begin by telling the reader how to play the game. But what if the reader does not know what mahjong is? You should not assume that the reader knows as much as you do about the topic. Learning about his or her background will help you determine what to include in your writing.

Because this class is a writing community, much of what you write in this course will be directed toward your class and your instructor. Your writing audience will be each other. As you write, you need to attend to the background of this special group.

To find out more about your classmates and your instructor, conduct a class survey. The instructor will divide the class into two or three groups. Have one member in your group complete the chart below, about skills, interests, education, and background. Write short answers to each topic. When the instructor has put all the group reports together (including the instructor's responses) to form a class-survey report, he or she will give each class member a copy of the report to use in the next exercise.

CLASS SURVEY: YOUR GROUP					
Topic	Name	Name	Name	Name	Name
Your country					
A special skill you possess					
Your major subject of study or interest to you					
Your main reason for studying English					
A special place you enjoy					
Who you live with					

Getting Ideas

BRAINSTORMING

Using the information from the full class-survey report and the T-shirts, discuss these questions with a group:

1. Were any of the answers on the survey surprising?
2. What is the most interesting thing you learned from the survey responses?
3. What interests do you share with your classmates?
4. What kinds of topics do you think your class likes to read about?

Next, look at the topics from the class-survey report and on the T-shirts. In choosing a topic for your own writing, think about a subject from the class-survey report that you know well and that you think your classmates would like to read about; or choose one topic about yourself that you included on your T-shirt. Discuss topic ideas with your group and with your instructor, keeping in mind that you will want to choose a topic that appeals to your audience, your classmates. Choose one topic for your next writing assignment.

My topic will be _____.

Composing

THE PARAGRAPH, ENGLISH-STYLE

In academic English, writing is organized into paragraphs. A paragraph is a small unit of writing that contains a single idea. The first line of each paragraph is indented. Each time you see an indented line in a composition, you know that a new paragraph has begun.

Writers of English organize their ideas in a direct way, normally beginning each paragraph with a sentence that presents the main idea of the composition. The main elements of a paragraph include the *topic sentence*, the main-idea sentence; the *support*, the sentences in the middle that give more details about the topic; and the *conclusion*. The length of the paragraph depends on the complexity of the topic.

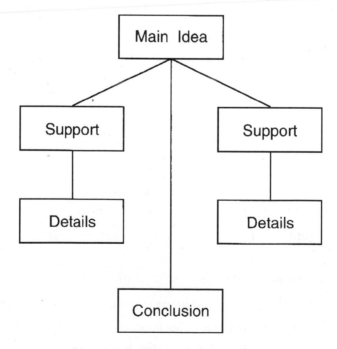

Diagram of a Paragraph, English-Style

Exercise 1.1   Read the following paragraphs, which were written by students. With a group, find the topic sentence, the support, and the conclusion. (Note that these paragraphs also have titles.)

My Best Quality

Being responsible is my best quality. I think I have to be responsible for everything I do in my life. For example, I graduated from the university in my country by myself. I didn't require the support of my parents. And before I came here, I worked at an automobile factory for about one year in order to earn the money to study English in the United States. Then, I saved enough money to be able to live on my own in the U.S. for one year. Responsibility is not only my quality, but also my policy and spirit.

Shoji Harada
Japan

My Father, My Hero

My father, a nice, fifty-year-old man, is the person whom I admire the most. From my childhood, he seemed to be a big tree. I could be protected perfectly by him. My father had such big and strong arms that he could hold me on the top of his head, and I could see whatever I wanted to in the crowded zoo. He was always my hero. But sometimes, I would think that he didn't love me anymore in my little and strange mind because I was punished for making some mistakes. Now, I know that he loves me. That's the reason that he wanted me to know what was wrong and right. I will always love and admire my father for these things.

Lin-Lee Chin
Taiwan

PARAGRAPH SUPPORT

Notice that in the paragraphs in Exercise 1.1 all the sentences relate to the topic sentence.

In "My Best Quality," the supporting examples tell how the writer is responsible. In "My Father, My Hero," the supporting details (which include an example) explain why the writer admires her father.

Supporting details in a paragraph explain, or show, why a topic sentence is true. All the support (such as examples, facts, descriptive details, or narrative details) relates to the one main idea expressed in the topic sentence.

Exercise 1.2 For each of the following topic sentences, write three possible supporting sentences that could be included in a paragraph. Afterwards, discuss your support for each topic sentence with your class to determine if it relates to each main idea.

1. Topic sentence: English is necessary in my life.

   Support: _____

   Support: _____

   Support: _____

2. Topic sentence: Laziness is one of my friend's bad qualities.

   Support: _____

   Support: _____

   Support: _____

3. Topic sentence: Living alone is worse than living with my family.

   Support: _____

   Support: _____

   Support: _____

PARAGRAPH TITLE

A one-paragraph composition should have a title to tell the reader the main idea of the writing. Usually, the title is not a sentence, but rather, a well-chosen word or phrase.

Paragraph Titles: **My Best Skill**
Living Alone

Exercise 1.3 The following is another paragraph written by a student. With a group, read it, and determine its main idea. Then, give the paragraph a title.

I am a forgetful person. Most people like to be clever. Some of them do very well. But I always make mistakes such as missing a bus, missing a class, and forgetting to take care of my possessions. I always forget the bus timetable. When I was at the university, I usually forgot the classes because they were at different times every day. Sometimes I couldn't get home because I lost my way. When I got home, I could not find my door key. Although I entered my house successfully, I sometimes forgot to take the key from the door lock. I think nobody is like me. Everybody in the world is clever and a genius, except me. But I like to be forgetful because that's the way I am.

Yongseo Park
Korea

CONCLUSION

In a one-paragraph composition, the topic sentence introduces the main idea, the supporting sentences explain the topic sentence, and a final sentence should provide a conclusion. The concluding sentence should close the paragraph by returning to the main idea of the topic sentence. One way that a writer can do this is to repeat or to rephrase a key word or idea that was expressed in the topic sentence.

In the paragraph-title exercise, notice how Yongseo Park returned to the main idea of the topic sentence in his concluding sentence.

> *Topic sentence:*   I am a **forgetful** person.
>
> *Concluding sentence:*   But I like to be **forgetful** because that's the way I am.

Look back at Exercise 1.1. What key word or idea does Shoji Harada include in both his topic sentence and his conclusion? What is the key word or idea that Lin-Lee Chin repeats in her concluding sentence?

THE FORM OF A PARAGRAPH

What should a paragraph look like? When you write a paragraph, you should follow some basic rules of format.

- Use 8-by-11-inch notebook paper.
- Leave a margin on the left- and right-hand sides.
- Leave a space at the top and the bottom of the page.
- Indent the beginnning of the paragraph.
- Do not break a paragraph by indenting a line in the middle of the paragraph. (A paragraph runs continuously from the first sentence to the last.)
- The figure on page 10 shows what a paragraph should look like on a page.

The Values of Friendship

Friendship is the most beautiful thing in life because you need people to talk to and to share some sentiments with. I don't think that all people know this they don't know how many things they can get from friends. They may lack something for example they might need somebody to talk to when they feel lonely. They may need some financial help at the end of the month to pay all their bills. Friends do many more things for you. Now you can know the real meaning of friendship.

Form of a Paragraph

Writing

A PARAGRAPH FOR THE CLASS

Write a paragraph on the topic that you chose on page 6 relating to your class survey or T-shirt.

Begin with a topic sentence that presents the main idea. Include support to explain the topic and a brief conclusion that returns to the main idea.

When you finish, give your paragraph a title.

Building Language Skills

SENTENCE COMPLETENESS

The sentence is the basis of written English. A sentence is a group of words with a subject and a verb, and it expresses a complete thought. It begins with a capital letter and ends with a period. When you write, it is important for you to be aware of where your sentences begin and end.

Examples:

The bird flew away.	Sentence (subject + verb; expresses complete thought)
The man in the street.	Not a sentence (no verb; not a complete thought)
After I graduated from high school.	Not a sentence (not a complete thought; does not tell what happened after graduation)

Exercise 1.4   Read each group of words below and decide if it is a complete sentence or not. If it is not a complete sentence, identify the missing element: a subject, a verb, or a complete thought.

1. When I lost my job.

2. I wanted to make a fresh start.

3. Interviewing for a job in a factory.

4. He was unable to return to school.

5. On the train saw a lonely woman.

6. Choosing a career is an important step.

7. Because my parents needed me, I stayed in my hometown.

8. The man who took photographs at the wedding.

Exercise 1.5   The following paragraph has no punctuation to show where sentences begin and end. Read the paragraph to yourself and listen for the natural pauses between two ideas. Look for subjects and verbs that form complete sentences. At the end of complete sentences, put periods, and at the beginning of sentences, add the necessary capitalization.

The Values of Friendship

Friendship is the most beautiful thing in life because you need people to talk to and to share some sentiments with I don't think that all people know this they don't know how many things they can get from friends they may lack something for example they might need somebody to talk to when they feel lonely, they may need some financial help at the end of the month to pay all their bills, friends do many more things for you, now you can know the real meaning of friendship

Mohammed Anasse El-Khadiri
Morocco

SENTENCE PATTERNS: WHO OR WHAT DOES WHAT?

Look at this complete sentence:

Example   **Children often like books about pirates.**

This is a complete sentence because it has a subject and a verb, and it relates a complete thought. This way of building an effective sentence is by using the Who or What Does What? model. In this pattern, the subject is the *doer* of the action in the verb.

Identify the subjects and verbs and notice how this model is used in the following sentences.

The alarm clock rings at 7 A.M. every morning.
My parents wanted me to study business.
Television brings us news quickly.

Exercise 1.6   Write sentences for the following subjects. Think about what the subject does or did or will do. That will be your verb.

Example   **The policeman**
(What did he do?)
The policeman arrested the drunk driver.

1. The elephant _____

2. The committee _____

3. My father _____

4. The ice cream _____

5. Prices _____

Exercise 1.7   Now, write subjects for the following verb phrases. Think about who or what does the action of the verb. Be sure your subject agrees with your verb.

Example   **_____ are flying south for the winter.**
(Who or what is flying south?)
The birds are flying south for the winter.

1. _____ gave a rose to his girlfriend.

2. _____ fell from the sky.

3. _____ has many interesting sights.

4. _____ bend in the wind.

5. _____ interrupted our meeting.

SENTENCE PATTERNS: SUBJECT + LINKING VERB + COMPLEMENT
Now, look at these sentences, and identify the subjects and verbs:

> My grandfather was a doctor.
>
> The beaches of Honduras look beautiful.
>
> My apartment is in a good area of town.

These sentences do not follow the Who or What Does What? model. In these sentences, the subject does not do anything; rather, it is *linked* with a complement, a word or words that complete the meaning of the subject.

This sentence pattern is Subject + Linking Verb + Complement. A complement may be one of these:

a noun phrase *(a doctor)*

an adjective *(beautiful)*

an adverb phrase of time or place *(in a good area of town)*

Exercise 1.8   With a partner, complete the paragraph below by adding appropriate subjects and verbs. Discuss whether the sentences you created follow the Who or What Does What? model or the Subject + Linking Verb + Complement pattern.

My Favorite Pastime

My favorite pastime _____ reading. Whenever I _____have_____ free time, _____ pick up a book and _____One_____. Reading _____ me in many ways. _____ gives me many oppportunities. A travel book _____ me on a trip through Africa or _____give_____ me the wonders of Peru. A history book _____teach_____ me how people lived in ancient Greece or why the Germans _____ against the French in World War II. When _____ read literature, I feel that I _____am_____ in the story. I _____am_____ to understand why a character _____try_____ the way he does. And I can _____ all human emotions: love, hate, pride, sorrow. Reading _____ many doors in my life. Clearly, _____ is a wonderful way to pass time.

Exercise 1.9   Write sentences for the following subjects on another piece of paper. Follow the Who or What Does What? model or the Subject + Linking Verb + Complement pattern.

1. The shy student . . .

2. The huge dog . . .

3. Jogging . . .

4. My best friend . . .

5. Sunday afternoons . . .

SIMPLE PRESENT TENSE

The simple present tense is the most commonly used verb tense in English. You can use this verb tense to express yourself in many writing situations:

- to tell general facts about a person

Example   **Nadia has brown eyes and curly hair.**

- to tell general facts about a place

Example   **Indonesia consists of thousands of islands.**

- to make a generalization

Example   **Most children obey their parents.**

- to present beliefs, preferences, or opinions

Example   **My friend Jim likes Thai food, but I don't.**

- to describe an everyday activity or habit

Example   **Every morning Val drinks several cups of coffee.**

- to express ownership

Example   **Gail has three cats.**

You can use the simple present tense to express general information and facts about yourself.

Example   I **want to study** graphic design at an American university.

Unfortunately, I **am** a very lazy person.

When you use this verb tense to describe another person or a place, or with any singular *he*, *she* or *it* subject, remember that the verb needs an *s* or *es* ending.

Example   John **works** at a pizza parlor.

Classical music **relaxes** me.

Exercise 1.10   The simple present tense will enable you to express general information and facts about yourself. Write sentences about yourself that give the information indicated below.

1. Tell about your appearance.

2. Make a generalization about your current living situation.

_____

3. Express a fact about your education.

_____

4. Tell about a belief that you have.

_____

Exercise 1.11   Use the topics below to find out information about a classmate, and then write sentences about him or her.

Tell about your classmate's appearance.

Example   *My classmate, Luis, has dark brown hair.*

1. Express a preference your partner has for a food item.

_____

2. Describe one of your partner's bad habits.

_____

3. Describe an everyday activity that your partner does.

_____

4. Tell about something your partner owns.

_____

SENTENCE PATTERNS: COORDINATION

Look at these sentences:

She talked to her parents. She didn't follow their advice.

She talked to her parents, but she didn't follow their advice.

Which of the sentences do you prefer? Why?

The third sentence may appeal to you most because the writer has combined the two ideas into one sentence to show how the ideas relate. One way to combine sentences is called coordination. The following coordinators are used to combine two complete sentences into one:

Addition	Contrast	Choice	Effect	Cause
and	but	or	so	for
	yet	nor		

Coordination in sentences shows the close relationship between two ideas. Look at the sentences below, which illustrate the meanings of each of the coordinating words given above.

Tim took the bus, and Albert walked home. (*and* = addition: idea 1 and
    Idea 1   Idea 2   idea 2 have equal importance)

Janet was tired, but she continued to work. (*but* = contrast: idea 2
    Idea 1   Idea 2   contrasts with idea 1)

We can see a movie, or we can go to the park. (*or* = choice: between ideas 1
    Idea 1   Idea 2   and 2)

BMWs are expensive, so few students own them. (*so* = effect: idea 2 presents
    Idea 1   Idea 2   the effect of idea 1)

Note: The word *for* is not commonly used for coordination today. It's more natural to use the word *because*, as the example sentences below illustrate.

Natural

Elizabeth bought Peter a gift **because** she loved him.

Less Common

Elizabeth bought Peter a gift, **for** she loved him.

Exercise 1.12   Use coordinators to combine the ideas in the paragraph that follows. Choose the coordinator that best shows the relation between the ideas.

My Daughter Nora

My daughter Nora is a loving person. She often leaves me notes that say "I care for you," _____ she tells me "I love you" many times a day. At night, I tell her several times to go to bed, _____ she continues to hug and kiss me for a long time. She has to wake up early, _____ I finally have to shout at her to go to sleep. Sometimes I visit her at school, _____ I watch her play. On the playground, she is either hugging her teacher, _____ she is holding hands with one of her friends. She tries to hold her sister, _____ her sister pushes her away. Her sister loves her, too, _____ she is not as affectionate as Nora is.

Exercise 1.13   Use an appropriate sentence coordinator to combine the pairs of sentences below. Consult the list of coordinators on page 15.

Example   **Juan often goes fishing. He never catches anything.**

               Juan often goes fishing, but he never catches anything.

1. We can go to the movies this afternoon. We can go to the park.

2. Zufan caught a cold. She stayed home in bed yesterday.

3. Tran takes the subway to school every day. He doesn't enjoy it.

4. Every weekend Shui visits the seashore. She eats fried clams.

5. On school days, Binh brings his lunch. He buys a hot dog from the street vendor.

PERSON IN WRITING

When you write about personal topics, you most commonly use *I, me,* or *my* (first person). Look at these sentences:

> **I am a forgetful person.**
>
> **My favorite pastime is reading.**

It is acceptable to use first person when you write about yourself and your experiences.

VOCABULARY: CHOOSING THE CORRECT WORD FORM

As you write in English, you will naturally spend time searching for words, in your head and in your dictionary. You will feel successful when you find the right word to express your meaning. But to write grammatically correct English, that is not always enough. You must also consider which form of the word to use in your sentence.

For example, you decide to write this sentence:

> **I am an <u>optimistic</u> person.**

Optimistic is an adjective that modifies the noun *person.* It tells what kind of person you are.

Note that *optimistic* must be changed if it has another function in a sentence.

> **With my <u>optimism</u>, I refuse to accept defeat.**

Optimism is a noun. It names the characteristic that you have. Now look at another form of the word.

> **If someone asks me how I will do on a test, I respond <u>optimistically</u>.**

Optimistically is an adverb. It modifies the verb *respond,* telling how you respond.

How will you know what the various forms of a word are? In English, there are several suffixes (word endings) that indicate whether the word is a verb, a noun, an adjective, or an adverb. As you build your vocabulary, you should become familiar with them. You can also look in a dictionary to find the correct form of a word.

Exercise 1.14   Practice using the correct word form in the following sentences.

1. generous   generosity   generously

   a. People always appreciate his _____.

   b. When I explained my problem to him, he _____ offered some advice.

   c. She made a _____ gesture by offering to help me paint my house.

2. friendly   friendliness

   a. Marsha is a very _____ woman.

   b. I see her _____ whenever she talks to strangers.

3. beautiful   beauty   beautifully

   a. The sun shone _____ when I awoke this morning.

   b. On my vacation, I enjoyed the _____ of the mountains.

   c. If you see a _____ sunset, you will remember it for a long time.

4. succeed   success   successful   successfully

   a. Your _____ in life depends on yourself.

   b. They _____ in tasks because they work diligently.

   c. A _____ person is one who achieves a goal.

   d. After Louis worked on the computer, it _____ printed the document.

5. responsibility   responsible   responsibly

   a. Dimos accepted his _____, and he returned to Greece to serve in the army.

   b. The tornado was _____ for the damage to my neighbor's roof.

   c. Cho handled the group assignment _____ by doing his share of the work.

6. create   creative   creation   creatively

   a. The book *Whack on the Side of the Head* shows readers how to think _____.

   b. The left side of a person's brain is supposed to give him or her the power to _____.

   c. The dress designer's latest _____ is a chiffon evening gown.

   d. Try to be _____ when you choose a writing topic.

7. interesting   interest

   a. An _____ quality of cats is their off-and-on affection.

   b. Do you have any _____ in going to graduate school?

Exercise 1.15   Look at the words that you chose to complete the sentences in Exercise 1.14. With a partner, complete the chart below, placing each word under the appropriate group. Then, underline the suffixes for the noun, adjective, and adverb forms. The first suffix is already underlined.

Noun	Adjective	Adverb	Verb
generosity			
	friendly		
		beautifully	
			succeed
responsibility			
	creative		
interest			

Revising

EVALUATING IDEAS

Exchange your "Paragraph for the Class" from page 10 with a partner. Read each other's papers. Do not correct each other's grammar or spelling, but focus on the content of the writing by answering these questions orally.

1. What do you like about the paper?

2. Would you like more information about any of the writer's points?

3. Is there any part that you do not understand?

Next, evaluate your partner's composition by using the Writing Checklist, which follows. Write comments in the margins of your partner's paper if any of the checklist points are not covered adequately. Discuss your comments with your partner. Use your partner's suggestions, and revise your paragraph.

Writing Checklist

1. Does the paragraph have a topic sentence that tells the main idea?
2. Does the paragraph contain a single idea?
3. Is the main idea supported?
4. Is there a concluding sentence?
5. Are the sentences complete?
6. Is there a title?
7. Is the paragraph indented?

Journal Writing

A journal is a book in which you write about your thoughts, your life, your studies, and your problems. It is a place in which you can reflect on yourself and the world around you. You should not worry about grammar or organization of ideas. Allow your thoughts to take control. By keeping a journal, you will discover ideas and find it easier to express these ideas in English.

In this class, you will use a journal to write on topics of your choice—any thought or problem or observation you wish to record. The journal will also be used as a place to reflect on your writing and on the topics you will encounter in this class. For example, the two topics below deal with the activities you have completed in chapter 1.

A.   In your journal, write a one-page entry on one of these topics:

1. Write about one interesting thing you have observed about someone in your class.

2. Write about one interesting thing you have learned from someone in the class.

B.   Write a one-page entry on a topic of your choice.

Use your past experiences, your present situation, and your hopes for the future to give you ideas for writing on your chosen topic. Make your journal unique!

Here is a list of possible topics:

1. My Parents and Their Lives

2. My Best Friend

3. My Most Frightening Experience

4. My Observations About My New Town (or City)

5. My Worst Habit

6. The Best Day of My Life

7. My Favorite Possession

8. My Trip to the United States

9. My Favorite Place

10. Reactions to a News Story (Book, TV Show, Movie, or Song)

11. Impressions of My Classmates (Teachers, or Classes)

12. My Goals

More Writing Topics

1. Write a paragraph that describes one quality of one member of your family.

2. Write a paragraph that explains what you hope to gain from this class.

3. Write a paragraph about an important person in the history of your country.

Chapter 2

Stories We Tell

Which member of your family is the best storyteller?

Did your parents or grandparents ever tell you a memorable story about you as a child?

Do you have a favorite folk story from your culture?

Family Stories

Getting Ideas

QUESTIONNAIRE: FAMILY EXPERIENCES

Read the questions below. With your class, discuss vocabulary. When you understand the questions completely, answer them by checking *Yes* or *No*.

QUESTIONNAIRE		
Have you, or anyone in your family, ever...	Yes	No
1. survived a dangerous experience?		
2. accomplished a nearly impossible feat?		
3. done or said something hilarious?		
4. been badly frightened by someone or something?		
5. given or received an unusual gift?		
6. had an adventurous time in the wild?		
7. had an embarrassing experience?		
8. had an unforgettable love experience?		
9. won an exciting competition?		
10. done a heroic act?		

BRAINSTORMING

Think of one memorable family experience. In a group, tell your story. Listen and comment as group members tell their stories.

Composing

TOPIC SENTENCE

Look at this sentence:

My summer vacation in the Bahamas was very relaxing.

The word *relaxing* describes the kind of experience the writer had. This sentence would be a good topic sentence for a paragraph. It introduces the topic, and it limits the topic by saying something specific about it. The information in the topic sentence that limits the topic is often called the controlling idea.

In the sentence above, the topic, "my summer vacation in the Bahamas," is limited by the controlling idea, "was very relaxing." The writer could have expressed a different idea about the vacation, such as "My vacation in the Bahamas was a disaster," but he or she decided to focus on how relaxing it was.

Look at these topic sentences:

A. My favorite teacher, Mrs. Hedayati, was a very serious person.

B. In my opinion, the changing job market will cause me many difficulties.

In example sentence *A*, what is the topic? What is the controlling idea?

In example sentence *B*, what is the topic? What is the controlling idea?

Exercise 2.1   Read the topic sentences below and identify the topic and the controlling idea.

Example   ***Living in Monterrey*** was ***the happiest time of my life.***
                        Topic   Controlling idea

1. Learning a foreign language can be fun.

2. Nonverbal communication takes several forms.

3. By following three steps, you can take a perfect picture.

4. Living alone has several advantages.

5. An effective teacher knows her subject, communicates her knowledge, and inspires her students to learn.

6. Women are more rational than men.

7. The Grand Canyon is one of the most beautiful sights in the United States.

8. Smoking should not be allowed in public areas.

Exercise 2.2   Read the following two paragraphs. With a partner, write a topic sentence for each paragraph.

_____

_____

During the sixty days of training, I had to lose pride and I was treated like a dog. I didn't need to say anything, just remember two words: "Yes, sir." Every day, from early morning to night, the terrible things never stopped. I could see some of my fellow soldiers fall down or throw up on the field after running 5,000 meters. Soldiers got sunstroke almost every day when we were training at noon under the biggest sun. The temperature was 95 degrees. At midnight I would suddenly wake up hearing somebody crying. I also had chances to see people commit suicide in the restroom because they couldn't stand the terrible training anymore. Of course, soldiers never stopped trying to escape. I was thinking what hell I was living when I saw these terrible things happen.

Lou Lee
Taiwan

_____

_____

It was a hot summer afternoon. My two older brothers and I were at home, with nothing much to do. Our family was moving, and two locker trunks sat in the living room waiting to be filled. It all began as a game. Eric, my oldest brother, said to me, "Laura, get in the trunk. I want to see if you fit." Being thirteen and trusting implicitly in my brother's judgment, I crouched down and squeezed into the trunk. Pleased with the game, Eric quickly closed the trunk. Total darkness surrounded me as I heard the two locks snap shut. "OK, Eric, I fit . . . you can let me out now," I called. "Come on, Eric, I can't breathe." Suddenly, I felt claustrophic, but worse, I sensed my brother's panic from outside. Something was wrong. Tears running down my face, I started screaming. My two brothers tried to calm me down telling me to save my breath. Five endless minutes passed in the suffocating trap before my other brother, John, broke the locks with a hammer. As I rose from the trunk, I collapsed in relief, but probably not with as much relief as Eric felt.

Note: The authors have omitted topic sentences of the above paragraphs for this exercise.

Writing

A FAMILY OUTING

Write a one-paragraph composition about a trip or outing you have taken. The trip could be a long vacation, or it could be a short outing—to the beach, for example. Identify and describe the place of your vacation so that your audience (a classmate and your instructor) will understand the setting.

Be sure to include a topic sentence, supporting details, and a concluding sentence. In your support, you may want to tell when the trip took place, what you did and saw, who went with you, where you went, how long you traveled, how you liked the trip, and so on.

Give your paragraph a title.

Revising

Exchange papers with a partner. Read and evaluate your partner's paragraph to make sure that it contains the essential elements: a topic sentence, support, and a conclusion.

Composing

PARAGRAPH UNITY

Each of the paragraphs in Exercise 2.2 tells a unified story about an experience. The paragraphs have *unity* because they contain only those ideas that tell the story. Moreover, all the supporting ideas in the paragraph relate to one particular idea about the experience: how the person felt or what kind of experience it was.

Look at the paragraphs again to see how all the sentences tell about the writer's feeling or about the type of experience he or she is describing.

A paragraph has *unity* when all of its sentences, including the topic sentence, support, and conclusion, relate to the same main idea. The main idea is expressed in the controlling idea of the topic sentence.

Read these example topic sentences:

New York City is a wonderful place to live.

New York City is a dangerous place to live.

How could writers using these topic sentences ensure that their paragraphs about New York are unified?

The writer of the first paragraph about New York should focus on the "wonderful" aspects of the city; the paragraph's unity will come from supporting ideas that all explain or show how the city is wonderful.

Which of these sentences would be appropriate for the first paragraph?

In New York, there are stores that sell everything you can imagine.

Housing is expensive in New York.

The writer of the second paragraph can write a unified paragraph if all the supporting ideas explain the dangerous side of the city. Which of the following sentences would be appropriate for the second paragraph?

Many people feel that it is unsafe to walk in Central Park late at night.

It's also difficult to find an apartment in New York.

Cars are often stolen or broken into on certain streets in New York.

Exercise 2.3 Read the paragraphs below. With a partner, draw a line through any sentences that do not support the main idea expressed in the topic sentence.

Violence on TV

Many television programs are too violent for children. For example, police stories such as *Law and Order* and *NYPD Blue* show crime and violence. Many times, these programs show people killing each other, using guns, knives, or cars. Children may watch these programs and begin to consider that violence is not so serious. Children may then go out and imitate the bad actions they have seen on television. In addition, many TV programs help children to learn early about sex. They may begin to have sex at an early age because of TV. In conclusion, children see too much violence on television, and they should not watch violent programs.

Walking in Houston

In Houston, you don't feel free to walk on the streets. I like walking and looking around very much, but, unfortunately, in this city, whenever I walk on the street, people look at my face as if I am guilty. That's because nobody else walks, and most people have their own cars. Perhaps I will buy a car next year. Right now I have too many bills and no job. When I walk, people drive by and turn their heads to stare at me. Even during the day, streets near my home look like ghost towns because nobody is walking outside. Only at night, a few guys come out, walk around, and drink a couple of beers. I sometimes wonder why people have to drink that much and commit crimes. All these facts make me feel less free when I walk in Houston.

Patience: A Characteristic of Good Teachers

Good teachers need great patience. Not all students are easy to teach. Because some students are lazy, teachers should have the patience to take care of them. They should push these students to learn. Also, some students study very hard, so teachers should be patient and impart more knowledge to them. Besides, good teachers had better know about a lot of things such as the universe, the world, and human life and its affairs so that they can speak very knowledgeably in class. If teachers have the characteristic of patience, their students will appreciate their efforts and learn more easily.

Writing

Think of one story that is remembered in your family because it has special meaning. The story can be about you or other members of your family. Identify members of your family so that your audience, your class, will see how these family members are related to you.

Write a paragraph about your family story. Begin with a topic sentence that tells how you or your family member(s) felt during the experience; or explain what kind of experience it was.

You may conclude by simply telling the final event in the story or by commenting about the importance of the story.

Building Language Skills

VOCABULARY: VERBAL ADJECTIVES

Memorable experiences like the ones you have just written about evoke strong feelings. At the time of the experience, perhaps you felt *joyous, humiliated, surprised,* or *angry.* Maybe the experiences themselves were *frightening, terrible,* or *happy.* Feelings and descriptions are often expressed by adjectives, like the words in italics.

Examine how adjectives are used in these sentences to relate feelings:

> I felt **frightened** when my car ran off the road.
>
> My sister had a very **embarrassing** experience—she fell off the stage during her high school play.

We often express feelings or descriptions through verbs used as adjectives. These verbal adjectives have two forms: one that ends in **-ed,** the other that ends in **-ing.**

The **-ed adjectives** are often used to describe how a person feels. The **-ing adjectives** can often describe the experience that produces that feeling.

Example I was **bored** last weekend. I had nothing to do.
(I felt boredom; I was bored.)

My weekend alone was **boring**.
(The weekend produced the boredom; it was boring.)

Common Verbal Adjectives		
relaxed	disappointed	humiliated
relaxing	disappointing	humiliating
confused	excited	surprised
confusing	exciting	surprising
depressed	frightened	tired
depressing	frightening	tiring

Exercise 2.4   On your own, think of one family story that tells a memorable experience that you or a member of your family had. Write down a word or two that tells how you or your relative felt during the experience. Then, write an adjective or two to describe the kind of experience it was. Write your words in the box below. Two example adjectives are provided.

How did you/he/she feel?	What kind of experience was it?
embarrassed	embarrassing

With a group or your class, share your words.

Exercise 2.5   Which words in the list of Common Verbal Adjectives above can tell how people feel? Which could describe an experience? Using verbal adjectives, write two sentences to show how you felt during one or two memorable experiences.

1. _____

_____

2. _____

_____

Using verbal adjectives, write two sentences that describe the experience or experiences. Share the best of your four sentences with the class.

1. _____

   _____

2. _____

   _____

PAST TENSE VERBS

Storytelling usually requires you to tell about something in the past. When you tell a story, you tell the main events of the story in the simple past tense. Other verb tenses are used to express past time, but these occur only in special situations. If you are in doubt about which tense to use when you write about the past, choose the simple past tense.

Examine the short paragraph below. Notice the use of past tense verbs to tell the story.

A Day at the Beach

When I went to the beach, I decided to go for a swim. The water was nice and warm. The waves were gentle, but high. I started to walk into the water. Then, I remembered that I could not swim, so I stayed where it was not too deep. The water was up to my thigh. The waves were not so high, so I stayed in the water for a while. Before I knew it, the undertow had pulled me deeper into the water. The waves were almost going over my head. I yelled for help. Luckily, my friends helped me out of the water. From that experience, I learned that I should not go in water that is too deep.

Maria Hernandez
Mexico

What verb tense is primarily used to tell the story in "A Day at the Beach"?

Look at this sentence:

Before I knew it, the undertow had pulled me deeper into the water.

What verb tenses are used here? Why?

Read this sentence:

The waves were almost going over my head.

What is this verb tense? Why do you think the writer used it here?

In the sentence, "Before I knew it, the undertow had pulled me deeper into the water," the writer uses "had pulled" (the past perfect tense: **had + past participle**) because this action came before her knowledge ("knew") of what was happening. In the sentence, "The waves were almost going over my head," the writer uses the past continuous tense (**was or were + -ing verb**) to tell about an action in progress at a particular time in the past. (The waves were going over her head at the time that the undertow had pulled her deeper into the water.)

Exercise 2.6   The following paragraph relates what happened in the Stan Laurel and Oliver Hardy film *Any Old Port*, in which the two play sailors on leave at a port. The writer began by telling the story in the past tense, so she should have continued with that verb tense. Some of the italicized verbs are correct and some are not. Edit the paragraph accordingly.

Any Old Port

The film "Any Old Port" *gave* an account of the lives of two sailors in a small port town. The film *started* telling what *happens* when Stan Laurel and Oliver Hardy *arrived* at a hotel. At this time, the hotel owner *is trying* to force a girl to get married to him. There *is* a funny moment when Hardy *tried* to sign the registration book. At that moment, the hotel owner *tries* to get a judge to marry him to the girl. While the judge *is leaving* the hotel, the girl *tried* to run away from the hotel owner. Unfortunately, the owner *had noticed* her action, and he *tries* to hit the girl. While Laurel and Hardy *played* pool, they *realized* that something *was* wrong. Then, they *saw* the hotel owner hide the girl in the storeroom. At that moment, they *start* fighting with him and *tried* to save the girl. The judge *arrives* to save the girl while they *struggled* to free her. Finally, after Laurel *had opened* the storeroom, the girl *escaped*.

Gloria Ruiz
Colombia

NARRATION AND GENERALIZATION

Past tense verbs are used to narrate, or tell, a story. However, as you tell the story, you may also present general facts or conditions. These are called generalizations, and they are expressed in the simple present tense.

One paragraph can contain different verb tenses. However, it is important to keep in mind which part of the paragraph is narration and which part is generalization.

Read these example sentences:

> **I took an examination to enter a Taiwanese university when I was 18, but I failed.**
> **It is difficult to enter a Taiwanese university.**

Which is part of the narration?

Which sentence is a generalization?

Exercise 2.7   Read the sample paragraph below. Pay close attention to the verb tenses that are used, especially to the past tense and the present tense verbs. Then, with a partner, answer the questions that follow:

A Terrible Experience

When I was a child, I had a terrible experience involving a dog. I think most children like dogs. Of course, I did, too. But when I was ten years old, one day I went with my family to a playground to exercise. Because I preferred to jog, I ran around the playground. While I was jogging happily, a dog suddenly ran up to me and started following me. That made me afraid, so I ran fast. The dog also ran fast and began to bark at me. I was even more afraid. I cried and screamed: "Ma! Ma!" Finally, my mother saved me. As a result of this experience, I hate dogs. Even now, when I see a dog nearby, or coming toward me, I always change my direction. I still remember that terrible day with the dog.

Chun-Min Chiou
Taiwan

1. Find sentences in the paragraph that tell the story. What verb tenses are used in these sentences? Why?

2. Find sentences in the paragraph that are not part of the narration. What verb tenses are used in these sentences? Why?

Revising

ORAL PEER REVIEW: EVALUATING TOPIC SENTENCE AND SUPPORT

Your peers, or classmates, are important sources of help to you in revising your writing. In an international class, you will find students with different language backgrounds. Each of you will encounter different difficulties and commonalities between your particular language and English. As a result, each of you has individual strengths in English. What may be difficult for you in English because of your native language may not be difficult to a classmate who speaks another language. These language differences make classmates with different languages good resources for your writing revision.

Oral review is a good way to begin a revision. If you read your paper aloud to a partner, he or she will focus on your ideas rather than on grammatical or mechanical mistakes. Revising your writing first for ideas and later for grammar, word choice, spelling, and so on will allow you to correct your own errors as you rewrite.

After you write your family story, read it to one or two classmates. Do not allow your partner(s) to see your paper. After you read your paper, have the partner(s) answer these questions:

1. Does the topic sentence tell how the person felt or what kind of experience it was?

2. Do the sentences all support the topic sentence?

SELF-EDITING

Now, using your partner's suggestions, revise your own paper. After you revise for content, you can self-edit your paper for grammatical and mechanical errors. Consider these questions:

1. Are the appropriate past tense verbs used?

2. Are present tense verbs used to relate general facts that are not part of the narration?

3. Are the appropriate forms of verbal adjectives used?

WRITING ASSIGNMENT 2

A Story from Your Country

Getting Ideas

READINGS: STORIES FROM OTHER COUNTRIES

Read these stories as a class, and discuss any unfamiliar words you find.

Djeha and the Onions
(North Africa)

Djeha was a poor man, but full of wits. One day, Djeha was stealing onions from his neighbor's field. His neighbor surprised him, and shouted at Djeha, "So you're the one who's been stealing my onions!" Djeha replied, "Don't jump to conclusions, neighbor. Don't be so hasty to judge me. You think I'm a thief just because I'm in your field?" "Oh, yes?" the man retorted. "So, tell me, then, what are you doing in my garden?"

Djeha looked up innocently at his neighbor, and explained that a strong wind had blown him over the fence and into the field. The neighbor eyed Djeha disbelievingly. "Then how did the onions get out of the ground?" "Well," Djeha replied, "the wind was so strong it was blowing me away. I was trying to hold onto something, so I grabbed the onions. I was holding them, and the wind pulled me up. They came right out of the ground!"

The neighbor was getting impatient with Djeha's story. He pressed Djeha even further: "Well, tell me, now, just how did those onions end up stacked so neatly in your pockets?" Djeha shook his head and put his hands on his hips. "You know, I was just wondering about that when you arrived."

The Dog and His Reflection
(Ancient Greece)

Once there was a dog in a village. He stole a piece of meat from a meat shop and ran off with it. He wanted to eat it at home. On the way home, he came to a narrow bridge over a stream. As he was crossing the bridge, he looked down and saw his own shadow in the water. He thought it was another dog, with a larger piece of meat than his. He tried to get that piece. He opened his mouth, and barked at the dog. However, the dog in the water was not a real dog, but his own reflection. So he dropped his own piece of meat into the water, and lost it. This story means "Grasp all, lose all."

Ya-Hui (Amy) Huang
Taiwan

BRAINSTORMING

In small groups, answer these questions about the stories:

1. What or who is the first story about? What does the story tell us about that topic or person?

2. "The Dog and His Reflection" ends with a moral, a sentence that explains the story's meaning. What does the sentence "Grasp all, lose all" mean?

3. Which of the two stories do you prefer? Why?

Composing

CONCLUSION

As you learned in chapter 1, a one-paragraph composition needs a good beginning and a good ending. The topic sentence states the main idea, and the concluding sentence returns to this idea.

Read this sample paragraph. What key word or idea is repeated in both the topic sentence and the concluding sentence?

Taiwan: A Small Country

It takes about five to six hours to drive a car from the top to the bottom of the small country of Taiwan. Taiwan is an island. Its area is one-eighth the size of Texas, and its shape is long, like a banana. If you drive a car, you enter the highway at Kiloun and leave the highway at Kaoshiung. In just five to six hours, you can finish this trip. If you take a plane from the north to the south, you take only fifty minutes. Within twelve hours, you can go around this island if you take a train. When you look at a big world map, you'll see that Taiwan is the size of the nail of your small finger. Although Taiwan is a big island, it is still a small country.

Eric Chi
Taiwan

Exercise 2.8   Read the paragraphs that follow. Add a concluding sentence to each paragraph.

Odessa: A Cultural Center

Odessa is one of the greatest cultural cities in the world. My city has a lot of museums: art museums with collections of many famous paintings, old and modern, Russian and foreign art, as well as historical, literary, and marine museums. There are also many colleges. The city has many theaters and movie houses, too. The opera and ballet theater, housed in a building designed by a French architect, is one of the most famous in the world. Moreover, my city is known to the world as a place where many very popular writers and humorists were born.

Stella Lisitsa
Ukraine

In general Odessa is one of the best cultural place, where
you can visit.

My Problems in Learning English

English is a difficult language for me to learn in two respects. First of all, vocabulary is a problem. This is because some words have almost the same meaning, and when you are writing or speaking you don't know which word you should use. For example, words like *thin, slender,* or *skinny* have really close meanings. How can you tell which word will be appropriate? Second, pronunciation is hard because my tongue can't make sounds like *th, y,* and *j*. This is because in my native language we don't have the *th* sound and also because we don't make any distinction between the *y* and the *j* sounds. It is very difficult for me to speak since people sometimes misunderstand what I am saying due to my incorrect pronunciation.

Carlos Castillo
Venezuela

So, Learning English is very hard but I can't do it.

Note: The authors have omitted the conclusion sentences in the previous paragraphs for this exercise.

Writing

COMPLETING A STORY

With a partner, read the beginning of the story "Crossing the River," and discuss a possible solution. Then, complete the story on the lines that follow. Tell the story in the past. Present your ending to the class.

Crossing the River

One day, a man had to take a wolf, a goat, and a cabbage across a river. However, his boat was very small, so it could hold only himself and one other thing. The man was confused. He did not know how he could take the wolf, the goat, and the cabbage over one at a time because the wolf wanted to eat the goat, and the goat wanted to eat the cabbage.

How did he do it?

Write your solution here:

First, the man took _____

_____

_____

_____

_____

_____

_____

_____

_____

Writing

A STORY FROM YOUR COUNTRY

With a partner, discuss stories from your country. Decide on a good story to tell. Write a first draft, or rough version, of the story on a separate sheet of paper. Use the suggested format that follows to organize your story. A short story may be told in one paragraph; a longer story may need two or more paragraphs.

The format is presented here in a simple outline form. In writing, outlines are used to "map out" the main contents of a composition. This outline will give you guidance about what information to put in each section of your story.

Title (Name of Story)

I. Introduction
   A. If needed, briefly give background information about the character and/or the story itself so that your audience will understand its importance.
   B. If background information is not needed, begin by naming the main character(s), his or her situation, and the first event of the story.

II. Support
   A. Tell the events of the story in the order in which they happened.
   B. Use one paragraph if the story is short.
   C. If the story is longer, divide the events into logical groups; each part will be one paragraph.

III. Conclusion
   A. Tell the final event of the story.
   B. If the story has a moral, add that at the end.

PAST TENSE VERBS

Review the past tense verbs presented in chapter 2, page 31, and complete the following exercise.

Exercise 2.9: With a partner, reread the two stories in Stories from Other Countries, on page 35. Discuss what verb tense predominates in both of these stories and why. Then, find the sentences below in the texts of the stories. With your partner, underline the past tense verb(s) in each sentence from "Djeha and the Onions." Be prepared to explain the use of each verb tense.

1. One day, Djeha was stealing onions from his neighbor's field.

2. Djeha looked up innocently at his neighbor, and explained that a strong wind had blown him over the fence and into the field.

3. "Well," Djeha replied, "the wind was so strong it was blowing me away. I was trying to hold onto something, so I grabbed the onions."

4. On the way home, he came to a narrow bridge over a stream.

5. As he was crossing the bridge, he looked down and saw his own shadow in the water.

VERB FORMS

One common problem that English learners have is using appropriate verb forms. In your grammar studies, you have by now learned many verb tenses in English. Once you have decided what time you are writing about, you need to use the correct form of the verb tense that fits.

Consult your grammar book or your instructor if you are unsure about the form of a verb.

Exercise 2.10 Read the paragraph below, in which the writer argues against premarital cohabitation. Underline the incorrect verb forms and correct them.

I think living together before marriage is irresponsible. Many people not take the marriage seriously. Then it can be make many problems for our society. For example, the children is not get a normal family and a couple is not mature. Many children becoming teenage criminals. They come from broken families. This problem discussed many times by experts because they think it is remarkable.

SENTENCE PATTERNS: MAIN + DEPENDENT CLAUSES OF TIME

Look at this sentence from "A Terrible Experience" on page 32.

When I was a child, I had a terrible experience involving a dog.

This sentence is complete because it contains a subject and verb and expresses a complete thought. To many students, this looks like two complete sentences because there are two sets of subjects and verbs:

        S   V   S V

When I was a child,   **I had a terrible experience involving a dog.**

Do both parts of the sentence express a complete thought?

When I was a child is a clause, a group of words with a subject and a verb, but it does not represent a complete thought. The time word *when* makes the reader expect more information about what happened "when I was a child." This part of the sentence is a dependent clause. It depends on the main clause (the other part of the sentence) to complete its idea.

In English, there are several types of dependent clauses. One of the most common types you will need to use is an adverbial dependent clause. An adverbial clause gives additional information about the action of the main clause: it can answer questions such as "When?" or "Why?" about the main-clause action, place a condition on the main-clause action, or show opposition between the dependent clause and the main-clause actions. An adverbial clause is introduced by a subordinator, a word like *when, if,* or *because.*

In this chapter, we will begin by looking at adverbial clauses that express time. This sentence pattern—main clause + dependent clause of time—is useful in narration.

Example   **When I looked up, I saw Manuel's face.**

               Sara ate her breakfast while she read the newspaper.

               After he had studied English for two years, Ali passed the TOEFL test.

               Chika hesitated before she gave her answer.

Here is a list of subordinators that introduce adverbial time clauses:

    when   while   after   before   as   until   as soon as   once   whenever

As the example sentences show, you should use a comma to separate the two clauses if the dependent clause comes before the main clause. Remember that the underlined part of each sentence above does not express a complete thought; thus, it cannot stand alone as a sentence.

Exercise 2.11   Choose a logical time subordinator from the above list to combine the pair of simple sentences below into a sentence with a main + dependent clause. Change the underlined sentence into a dependent clause. Add the appropriate punctuation.

1. I found a dollar on the street. I was walking downtown.

2. I finish my homework. I can go to the movies.

3. I wake up in the morning. I always take a shower.

4. I will not talk to you. You say you are sorry.

5. I eat ice cream. I feel a sharp pain inside my head.

VOCABULARY: WORD FORMS

In chapter 1, you saw that certain word endings (or suffixes) are used when a word has different functions in a sentence. For example, you recognized that *-ity* and *-ness* are noun suffixes. You also practiced using the correct form of a word in sentences. The next time you write, try to be aware of the importance of using the correct forms of words.

● **Exercise 2.12**   Read the following sentences. Identify any errors in word form and make corrections above each line.

> *Example*   **important**
>   **The most ~~importance~~ part of learning a language is attitude.**

1. When I promise someone I will do something, I try my best to do it perfect.

2. If I borrow a car from my friend, I should drive it carefully so that I don't destruction it.

3. If a teacher has intelligent, he will handle a difficult situation with skill.

4. Being a good teacher is difficulty.

5. A good teacher must have responsible to students.

6. Students aren't fear of the teacher.

7. Throughout his live, he fought against prejudice and discrimination.

Revising

To ensure that your story about your country on page 39 contains the essential parts, check your paragraph before you hand it in by answering the questions on the Writing Checklist, below.

Writing Checklist

1. Does the topic sentence briefly give background information about the story from your country? Does it introduce the topic and the controlling idea?

2. Do all the sentences relate to the topic?

3. Do the events follow in a logical order?

4. Are the correct forms of the past tense verbs used?

5. Are the correct word forms used?

Journal Writing

A. Write a journal entry on one of these topics:

1. Write about a moral or belief that guides your life.

2. Choose a saying or proverb from your culture, and explain its meaning.

    Example   **A bird in the hand is worth two in the bush.**

B. Write a one- to two-page entry on a topic of your choice.

More Writing Topics

1. Write a paragraph about a memorable experience that you had in a new city or country.

2. Write a paragraph about your trip to the United States.

3. Write a paragraph about a story you read in a book or magazine or a movie you saw.

Chapter 3

Decisions

What important decisions have you made so far in your life?

How do you feel when you have to make an important decision?

A Letter of Advice

Getting Ideas

READING

Read the composition and answer the questions that follow.

My Big Dilemma

Graduation day is near. Of course, everyone is happy to see an end in sight, and most of my friends are excited about their futures in their chosen areas. But right now, I feel very confused about my future. I must decide whether to return to Malaysia and help my father with his business, or stay here and do what I really want to do. This is a difficult choice between two very different paths. Time is running short.

I came to the United States four years ago to study in an American university. My parents agreed to let me come here if I promised to return to Malaysia after my studies and run my father's import-export business. At that time, I wanted so much to have the opportunity to study English and to live in the United States that I promised them anything. Besides, I thought that after four years in the U.S., I would be ready to work in my father's business. Now, I must make a serious decision. Either I return at the end of this year, or I'll risk losing my good relations with my family.

I have almost completed my undergraduate degree in English. I have worked very hard and I feel a tremendous sense of pride and achievement. My professors are so pleased with my work that they have encouraged me to continue my studies and get a master's degree in English literature. I am eager to go to graduate school and continue my learning and discovery.

A master's degree will take me another two years to complete. One of my professors says that I can get a position as a teaching assistant, so I won't have to depend on my parents for much financial help. I know that if I stay here longer I can learn more by practicing in my major. Once I get a master's degree in English, I will be able to get a good position teaching English in a Malaysian university. Then I can use the knowledge and skills I have learned here in the U.S.

The problem is my family. My father is getting old and his health is not good. He wants to train me to take over the business. I'm the only son. My oldest sister is a doctor, and my other sister is married with three children, so neither of them can help my father. My mother thinks I am selfish and irresponsible if I stay in the U.S. and continue my studies. No one in my family understands that I am not interested in being a businessman. In my culture, as a son, I'm supposed to run the family business, but my dream is to be a teacher in a university.

My American friends here all tell me that I should follow my dreams. They say that my parents will understand and will be happy when they see my success. Unfortunately, they do not really understand the Malaysian sense of responsibility and duty to one's family. If I do not keep my promise and help my family, how will I be able to face them?

Being torn between two very different paths is not easy. Whichever road I look down, I see good and bad; I see some happiness and some pain or disappointment. I know I have to choose one way and learn to be content with that decision.

Chi-Feng Chen
Malaysia

Discussion

1. What is your initial reaction to the situation described in "My Big Dilemma"?

2. Why is the story called "My Big Dilemma"?

3. What is Chi-Feng's situation at the university? What are his family's feelings about Chi-Feng's staying in the U.S.?

4. Discuss the reasons Chi-Feng gives for why he should stay in the U.S.

5. Discuss the reasons he gives for why he should return to Malaysia.

6. In your view, what should he do? What would you do?

7. Do you have a similar dilemma in your life—a dilemma in which your family's wishes and your wishes conflict? Explain your dilemma briefly to your group if you want to.

Writing

A LETTER OF ADVICE

Read "My Big Dilemma" again. Write a short letter of advice to tell Chi-Feng what he should do. After you finish, share your letter with a partner and compare your ideas. You may want to begin this way:

Dear Chi-Feng,

I'm a student at _____. We have not met, but I would like to offer you some advice about your situation. _____

_____

_____

_____

_____

_____

_____

_____

_____

Good luck!

                                         Sincerely yours,

                                         _____

Building Language Skills

MODAL AUXILIARIES

Read these sentences, which were taken from "My Big Dilemma":

> **I <u>must decide</u> whether to return to Malaysia and help my father with his business, or stay here and do what I really want to do.**
>
> **I <u>can get</u> a position as a teaching assistant.**
>
> **My American friends here all tell me that I <u>should follow</u> my dreams.**
>
> **I know I <u>have to choose</u> one way and learn to be content with that decision.**

Each of the sentences taken from the story contains a modal auxiliary verb that changes the mode, or meaning, of the main verb. With your class, discuss the meanings of the underlined verbs in the sentences above.

There are two kinds of modal auxiliaries: one-word modals and phrasal modals.

Modal Verb Forms			
One-Word Modals		Phrasal Modals	
can/could may will/would should must might	} + Base Form of Verb	be able to be allowed to be going to ought to/be to supposed to/ had better have to	} + Base Form of Verb

Note: The one-word modal *might* has no corresponding phrasal modal. *Might* usually gives the meaning of possibility in the present or future. Look at the following sentence.

Chi-Feng might go to graduate school.

It could be rewritten as:

It is possible that Chi-Feng will go to graduate school.

Also, note that one-word modals often have different meanings from the corresponding phrasal modals listed above. For example, look at these sentences:

Chi-Feng may go to graduate school.

You can see the director now.

Here, *may* shows possibility, and *can* shows permission.

Exercise 3.1   Edit the paragraph below by marking corrections above each line. Some of the forms of the modal verbs, in italics, are correct, and some are not. Discuss your corrections with a partner.

My Reasons for Coming to the United States

Why am I in the United States studying English? There are two reasons. First, I came here because I *have improve* myself. As a child in Saudi Arabia, I *could not to study* English because I hated it a lot. However, when I grew up, I decided that I *couldn't stayed* at the same stage of knowledge. I *had to go* out and see the world. Then, I *would getting* more information about the cultures and lifestyles of other countries. I chose to come here and study English because it is a popular language that people *should know*. Second, I came to the United States to help my father. He has a trade company in the U.S.A. which *must has* people who *can speaks* English. He thought I *ought come* here. Actually, I do not want to work in that company, but if I had said "No," I *would not be* here at all. I am not sure if I *will becoming* a supervisor in my father's company, but I am happy to be here studying English.

Exercise 3.2   Complete the following sentences with an appropriate modal verb form. There may be more than one acceptable answer.

Example   **Chi Feng is unhappy about having to return to Malaysia, but he ought to/should return to his country anyway.**

1. Chi-Feng has a difficult choice; it _____ help him to consult an older friend.

2. I _____ talk to him about my ideas when I see him next.

3. Chi-Feng's parents _____ understand his desire to continue his education when he talks to them directly.

4. If Chi-Feng returns home, he _____ readjust to life in Malaysia.

5. If he goes back to Malaysia, he _____ apply for a part-time teaching job so that he can follow some of his dreams.

6. He _____ think about the decision carefully before he acts.

7. I hope Chi-Feng _____ be happy with his decision.

VOCABULARY: INTRODUCING OPINIONS

To express your opinion in writing—in a letter of advice or in any type of persuasive writing—you can use introductory phrases like *in my opinion* to mark a statement as opinion, rather than fact. It's also possible to use certain verbs to indicate that you are presenting an opinion.

Example   **In my opinion, Chi-Feng belongs in Malaysia with his family.**

I *feel* that Chi-Feng should stay in the U.S.

Here are some common phrases and verbs used to introduce opinions.

Introductory Phrases	Verbs
In my opinion	believe
In my view	feel
As I see it	think

Exercise 3.3   Give your opinion about the topics below. For each one, use a different verb or phrase to show that this is an opinion.

Example   **What should the drinking age be?**

In my view, the drinking age should be twenty-one.

or

I believe that teenagers should be allowed to drink when they are eighteen years old.

1. Should couples live together before getting married?

2. Should foreign-student tuition be higher than tuition for residents?

3. What should the speed limit be on the highways?

4. Should money be spent on space exploration?

5. Should smoking be allowed in public areas?

WRITING ASSIGNMENT 2

An Important Decision

Getting Ideas

FREEWRITING: A GOOD ADVISER

Freewriting is quick writing about whatever comes to mind. This type of writing is used to help writers generate ideas for later writing.

To give you ideas for your next writing assignment, think of one person who helps you whenever you have a problem. Who is it? Why is this person so helpful? When did this person help you solve a problem or problems?

Write for three minutes about this person. Do not worry about form or grammar. Simply write what comes into your mind about this person and the times he or she helped you. Write without stopping during this short time. When you finish, read over what you have written. Then, write for another three minutes about the same subject: your good adviser.

Composing

TOPIC SENTENCE: PREDICTING CONTENT

Paragraphs need a clear focus just as sentences do. Look at the topic sentences that follow to see how the focus of a paragraph can change, depending on the controlling idea, what is said about the topic.

Examples of topic sentences:

Topic   Controlling idea

When my friend Yuki decided to get married, she ignored her parents' advice.

Topic   Controlling idea

When my friend Yuki decided to get married, she chose a man who respected her.

What would you expect to find in a paragraph that began with the first topic sentence? with the second topic sentence?

In the first paragraph, the reader would expect to find information that would answer questions like these:

Who did she decide to marry?

What was her parents' advice?

What did they say or do?

Why did Yuki ignore their advice?

What happened?

In the second paragraph, the reader might expect to find information like this:

Who did Yuki decide to marry?

What was he like?

In what ways did he show his respect for her? What specific actions did he do to show that he respected her?

How does Yuki feel about him?

As you can see, the controlling idea controls the content of the paragraph.

Exercise 3.4   Read the topic sentences below. Under each sentence, write questions relating to the information you would expect to find in a paragraph that began with this topic sentence. Compare your questions with a partner's.

1. When my boyfriend moved to another city, I decided to follow him.

   _____

   _____

   _____

2. Right now I have to choose a car that will fit my needs.

   _____

   _____

   _____

3. Even though I like living alone, I've decided to get a roommate.

   _____

   _____

   _____

4. I thought I was in love with my girlfriend, but after doing a lot of thinking, I knew it was time to break up with her.

_____

_____

_____

5. It's important for me to stay in the United States and get my bachelor's degree even though my wife and baby are in India.

_____

_____

_____

SUPPORT IN A SAMPLE PARAGRAPH

Now, look at how the first topic sentence (on page 51) about Yuki is developed into a paragraph. Note how the supporting sentences answer most of the questions that were anticipated earlier.

Yuki's Marriage Choice

When my friend Yuki decided to get married, she ignored her parents' advice. Yuki had been dating her boyfriend, Nobi, for nearly a year. They were both very much in love and wanted to get married. Unfortunately, her parents did not think he was suitable. Nobi adored Yuki, but he didn't have much money. Also, his social status was lower than Yuki's family's, and he lacked clear goals about his future. Yuki's parents wanted her to have an important position in their family business when she graduated from the university. However, Nobi didn't like this idea; he was proud and did not want his wife to work. Yuki thought for a long time about the situation. Her parents told her that if she married Nobi, she would not have a successful life. They were angry that she would give up her important status and her business opportunity. Nevertheless, Yuki finally decided that she loved Nobi so much that a profession, money, and status did not matter. She married him despite her family's objections. In the end, however, her parents discovered that Nobi was a worthy man. They accepted him and the marriage, and even gave him a position in their business.   *main idea sentence*

COHERENCE: ORDERING OF IDEAS

The writer of "Yuki's Marriage Choice" has provided the information the reader expects from the topic sentence and has included nothing irrelevant. The paragraph, thus, has unity. Moreover, she has ordered the ideas in "Yuki's Marriage Choice" in a logical way. In other words, it is easy for the reader to follow the writer's progression of ideas:

- Yuki's and her boyfriend's feelings toward each other
- a description of Yuki's boyfriend

- the parents' objections to the marriage
- Yuki's reaction and decision
- the final result.

Because it is easy to follow, "Yuki's Marriage Choice" has another important characteristic of a good paragraph: *coherence*. A *coherent* paragraph contains sentences that are logically ordered and that flow smoothly. In this text, you will discover ways of achieving coherence in your writing.

One mistake writers sometimes make is to put sentences in the wrong order. While writing, they might remember something they wanted to say earlier and include it in the wrong place. Or they might simply forget to reread the sentences they have already written and lose the logical connection between ideas. The result is an incoherent paragraph. If a paragraph has no coherence, it is difficult for the reader to understand the flow of ideas, and, thus, difficult to understand the main idea. *Coherence*, like unity, is an essential element of a well-written paragraph.

Exercise 3.5   With a partner or alone, read the following paragraphs, in which one or more sentences are out of order. Revise the paragraphs to make them more coherent by putting the sentences in the logical order. Use a separate piece of paper.

The Way I Think of Women

(1) An incident that happened to me in my middle school days changed the way I think of women. (2) I was 14 years old and I had a discussion with a female classmate. (3) She called me a *$!#%!! and a #$&*@!!! (4) A woman had never called me names like that, and that was not all. (5) Before this experience, I used to think of women as delicate flowers not to be touched, like petals of a rose. (6) In spite of this experience, I do not hate women; I have a girlfriend. (7) But since then, I do not look at women as made of soft material. (8) She hit me with her fist and that was more than I could stand, so I slapped her face. (9) I now look at her and other women realistically.

My Proud Moment

(1) An event in my life that has a special place in my mind occurred many years ago during a dog show in my country. (2) I love dogs, and at this time I used to have a big, smart, and beautiful purebred female Weimaraner. (3) Sometimes I went to dog shows with my dog. (4) One time I was invited to show my dog in a special event because she had won a first prize in the previous dog show. (5) My dog was a huge, tall, and strong animal weighing 85 pounds, and my niece was a thin, seven-year-old girl, weighing only 50 pounds, so it was not an easy task. (6) I was preparing my dog for this event. (7) The day before, my niece came to visit me from Venezuela, where she lived. (8) She loved my dog and I told her if she wanted to show the dog she could. (9) She accepted, and I taught her some things about training in the field. (10) Finally, she was ready for the show. (11) It was a memorable and exciting moment for me because when they, my niece and my dog, went to the field, everybody clapped for a long time. (12) It was a very proud moment for me.

A Casual Date

(1) In casual dating, the couple can behave in a relaxed way. (2) They can each dress casually. (3) When the man or woman arrives at the date's house, he or she might just honk the horn to tell the date that it's time to go. (4) The man doesn't have to worry about arriving on time or bringing a gift. (5) The woman does not need to put makeup on, because she prefers to look natural. (6) The man doesn't have to shave and wear cologne. (7) At the restaurant, they can eat fast or slowly, without thinking about formal etiquette. (8) The couple is free to speak about any subject and to laugh loudly. (9) They can wear jeans, T-shirts, or shorts. (10) On a casual date, the couple can be natural and relaxed in everything.

COHERENCE: TRANSITIONAL EXPRESSIONS

Another way to achieve coherence within a paragraph is by using transitional expressions. Transitions are words or phrases that connect clauses and sentences so that there is a smooth flow between ideas. They act as signals, showing the reader the relation between ideas.

Exercise 3.6   Look at the paragraph that you corrected in Exercise 3.1, and underline the words or expressions that you think are transitions. The first one is done for you.

My Reasons for Coming to the United States

Why am I in the United States studying English? There are two reasons. First, I came here because I have to improve myself. As a child in Saudi Arabia, I could not study English because I hated it a lot. However, when I grew up, I decided that I couldn't stay at the same stage of knowledge. I had to go out and see the world. Then, I would get more information about the cultures and lifestyles of other countries. I chose to come here and study English because it is a popular language that people should know. Second, I came to the United States to help my father. My father has a trade company in the U.S.A. which must have people who can speak English. He thought I ought to come here. In fact, I do not want to work in that company, but if I had said, "No," I would not be here at all. I am not sure if I will become a supervisor in my father's company, but I am happy to be here studying English.

Once you have finished, with a partner discuss what kind of relation you think each transition signals. In other words, does it show a relation of time, cause and effect, contrast, or something else? For example, the word *first* is a transition word of time.

In English there are several kinds of transitions. Words and phrases like *first, however*, and *for example* are transitional expressions. These expressions usually come at the beginning of a sentence, and they signal a particular relationship with the idea(s) in the previous sentence. When you use a transitional expression, you must put a period or a semicolon between your two sentences and a comma after the transition:

sentence.   **Transitional expression,**   sentence.

sentence;   **transitional expression,**   sentence.

Examples   **I wanted to learn English. Therefore, I decided to come to the United States to study.**

              My father wants me to work in his company; however, he will not force me to.

Here is a list of common transitional expressions, grouped according to their purpose:

Purpose	Transitional Expressions
To add an idea	in addition, furthermore, also, moreover
To show time sequence	first, second, next, then, last, finally
To contrast	however, in contrast, on the other hand
To show result	as a result, therefore, consequently
To emphasize	in fact, indeed, certainly
To show an example	for example, for instance, in particular
To generalize	in general, in short
To conclude	in conclusion, in summary, in short

Exercise 3.7   Add appropriate transitional words or phrases to the paragraph below.

My Ideal Job

In the future, I hope I can get an ideal job, which has three main characteristics. _____first_____, I would like to get a job with which I can earn a lot of money in a short time because money is necessary to live and to buy the things that I want. If I were rich, I could buy anything I wanted, and I could travel around the world whenever I had enough time. _____second_____, I want to use mechanical tools in my job simply because I like to touch and watch any mechanical object. _____for example_____, mechanical jobs are related to one of my hobbies, which is playing with radio-controlled cars. _____finally_____, I really don't want to work all day. So I'm going to find a job that can allow me to work only part time. If I don't have to work so long, I can have more time to do whatever I want, like watching movies. _____However_____, even though I know that finding an ideal job is hard, I will never give up until I get my ideal job.

Satoru Kato
Japan

Exercise 3.8 Combine the following sentences, using appropriate transitional expressions.

Example **Learning a new language demands a lot of patience.
It requires the ability to take risks.**

*Learning a new language demands a lot of patience.
Moreover, it requires the ability to take risks.*

*Learning a language demands a lot of patience; moreover, it
requires the ability to take risk.*

1. I had planned to fly to Brazil for my vacation. *however*
   I couldn't find a reasonably priced ticket.

   _____

2. I couldn't afford the trip to Brazil. *so*
   I decided to go to Mexico, which is a lot closer.

   _____

3. My travel agent found me a package deal at a great price. *in fact*
   This package will save me $500.00 for a ten-day trip.

   _____

4. Now I have to make some preparations for the trip. *also*
   I must get a new camera.

   _____

5. I am still disappointed that I can't go to Brazil.
   I am looking forward to seeing Mexico.

PARAGRAPH SUPPORT: ADDING DETAILS

In a paragraph, the support explains the main idea of the topic sentence. Supporting details may be facts, examples, statistics, or narrative events—depending on the writing assignment. The more specific the supporting detail is, the better it will explain and show your main idea.

Look at this topic sentence:

My job as a bookkeeper in an office was boring.

The reader asks,

What were your responsibilities as a bookkeeper?
What about the job was boring? or *Why were you bored?*

The writer might continue,

My job as a bookkeeper in an office was boring. All day long, I filed papers and typed letters. Often, I sat at my desk and watched the clock because I had no work to do.

These sentences illustrate what about the job was boring. The details explain the topic sentence and keep the reader interested. They show the reader why the job was boring.

Just as it is necessary to provide details to support your topic sentence, it is also important to give information to explain each of your major supporting points in a paragraph. In other words, you should add specific details throughout your paragraph.

Read the example paragraph below. What details could the writer add? Are there any Who? What? When? Where? Why? or How? questions you might want to ask? Write these questions in the places where the writer could add this information.

Quitting My Job

Two years ago, I quit my job in a clothing company in Japan because I didn't want to spend my whole life working at the same job. When I was an employee in this company, I wanted to change my life because I wanted to try other possibilities. At this time, I had worked for the company for three years. I had a good position, and the work was very easy for me. However, I didn't want to work in this company all my life. Japanese employees rarely quit a company. They work for just one company their whole lives. But it was a boring life to me. Consequently, I quit the company, and I'm now living in the United States. It's a big change for my life. Before, I didn't know a lot about another country, but now I'm learning about another culture. I am studying English.

Ryo Sano
Japan

When you read Ryo's paragraph, you might have asked the writer these questions:

What was your position in the company?

What city was the company in? Was it a big company?

What work was "very easy" for you?

Why was it "a boring life"?

What do you mean when you say this was "a big change for my life"? What have the consequences been?

Here is how Ryo might have revised his paragraph:

Quitting My Job

Two years ago, I quit my job in the Mitsui Clothing Company in Osaka, Japan because I didn't want to spend my whole life working at the same job. I was an accountant in this company, but I wanted to change my life because I wanted to try other possibilities. At this time, I had worked for the company for three years. I had a good position, and keeping the accounts was easy for me. However, I didn't want to work in this company all my life. Japanese employees rarely quit a company. They work for just one company their whole lives. But it was a boring life to me because all I did all day long was enter numbers into account books. Consequently, I quit the company, and I'm now living in the United States. It's a big change for my life. Before, I didn't know a lot about another country, but now I'm learning about another culture. I am studying English, and I might study engineering technology at the university. In fact, I may change to this field and start a new career.

The added details, which are underlined, give the reader more information about Ryo's situation. They make the reader understand Ryo's decision better. They also make the story more interesting.

Exercise 3.9   Read the following paragraphs. With a partner, mark places in the paragraphs where the audience will need more information. Below each paragraph write questions the reader will want answered.

A Job or an Education

When I finish my English studies, I'm going to make a difficult decision. It's about whether I will stay in the United States longer or go back to Mexico. I have a great opportunity to get a good job in Monterrey, Mexico, but if I learn English, I can have something much better. That's why I came to Houston. I'd like to continue studying after my English classes because some people tell me that maybe in the future I can be an international lawyer. I've been thinking a lot about this, and I know it is going to be very hard to make a decision. I have a good chance to study in the United States, but I will miss my country, my friends, my family, and, of course, my language.

Leticia Herrera
Mexico

1. _____

2. _____

3. _____

A Choice About My Education

The most difficult decision in my life was three years ago when I finished college and my professor asked me if I would like to study in Japan. He had a scholarship for me in Japan. That was the dream of my life, but my parents told me "no" because they had an idea that the family should be a unit. My boyfriend told me if I went, when I came back, I wouldn't have a boyfriend. It was a big decision because I wanted to know Japan, but my family didn't like the idea.

Beatriz O'Hara
Mexico

1. _____

2. _____

3. _____

Writing

Write a paragraph about an important decision you have made in the past or will make in the future.

Follow these steps.

1. To begin a paragraph about this decision, write a topic sentence. Your topic sentence should state what the decision was or will be, and then it should say something about the decision.

Topic
Example topic sentence: **My decision to quit my job and go back to school**

Controlling idea
was the wisest choice I have made in my life.

2. The support for your paragraph should relate to the specific idea expressed in the controlling idea part of your topic sentence. Some questions you might answer in the support part of your paragraph include the following:

- What events took place during your decision-making?
- How did you feel during and after the decision-making?
- What is your situation now?
- What factors helped you decide?
- What were the consequences of your decision?

3. You may want to conclude by restating your topic sentence or by stating your situation now, as a result of the decision. Concluding sentences can take many forms, depending on the type of writing you're doing. In a one-paragraph composition, the conclusion section is usually one or two sentences.

Example concluding section: **In conclusion, I have never regretted my choice to quit my job and return to the university. This decision has had a great impact on my life.**

Building Language Skills

SENTENCE FOCUS

Look at the following sentences:

John decided to go to medical school when he was very young.

John's decision to go to medical school was made when he was very young.

Which sentence is clearer and easier to understand? Why?

The first one is more effective because it tells us clearly Who Did What. In this sentence, the subject is personal rather than abstract. We are focused on a personal subject (John) and what he did (decided). In the second, we are focused on an abstract subject (John's decision). In English, we generally prefer personal or concrete subjects, which perform the action of the verb, rather than abstract or vague subjects, which do not perform an action.

Now look at these sentences:

There are several ways in which parents may influence their children.

Parents may influence their children in many ways.

Which sentence is clearer? Why? Discuss your answer with the class.

The subject of each sentence influences how the rest of the sentence should be written. It is also the focus for the sentence. Therefore, it's important for you to choose the most appropriate subject. When you are writing, think about what or who you are writing about, and try to make that the subject of your sentence.

Exercise 3.10   Read the following sentences, which are awkward and sometimes ungrammatical because they do not start with the most appropriate subjects. Using the logical subject, rewrite the sentences to make them clearer.

> *Unfocused:*   **The decision of the committee was to restrict smoking.**
>
> *Focused:*   **The committee decided to restrict smoking.**

1. Unfocused: In my country has many interesting superstitions.

   Focused: _____

2. Unfocused: Their feeling is romantic and happy.

   Focused: _____

3. Unfocused: Everything is really different in each country if we talk about weddings.

   Focused: _____

4. Unfocused: Punctuality of a good teacher in any school is important.

   Focused: _____

5. Unfocused: There is a complaint frequently made by teachers that children do not use their creativity.

   Focused: _____

6. Unfocused: In the course of life exist many important decisions that people have to take.

   Focused: _____

7. Unfocused: It will be required that students take final exams.

   Focused: _____

8. Unfocused: There are a lot of disagreements between me and my father.

   Focused: _____

9. Unfocused: What every person that has a TV watches is the news.

   Focused: _____

VOCABULARY: CHOOSING NEW WORDS

Another way you can make your writing more interesting is by using new words. Don't use the same words again and again in your writing.

Look at this short passage from a student's paragraph:

Being a teacher is the best profession for me. In my native country, Russia, I studied mechanical engineering. First, I worked in a plant for ten years as a designer. After that, I worked in a technical college for twenty years. I loved my job as a teacher because I loved my students. I didn't teach my students just a profession. I loved to tell them about all the things I had learned in life. Teaching was very rewarding to me.

Here, the student repeats the word *worked* and *loved* three times in this part of her paragraph.

Could she have used other words to say the same idea?

The writer could have said, "I taught in a technical college for twenty years."

She might have written, "I adored my job as a teacher because I loved my students" or, "I enjoyed telling them about all the things. . . ."

Exercise 3.11   In the following paragraph, the writer overuses the words *friends, friendly, a lot of,* and *make*. With a partner, choose new ways to express some of the repeated words in the paragraph. Use a dictionary if needed. Write your corrections above each line.

My Best Quality

Being friendly is my best quality. I'm so friendly that I can get a lot of friends very easily. When I go

out, I always make friends. For example, I like to go to a club named the Ocean Club. Every time I go

there I make a lot of friends. Finally, all my friends admire me because they say it's easy for me to make

friends. Being friendly is the quality that everyone wishes to have.

Rosario Garcia
Mexico

VOCABULARY: FORMALITY

When people speak, they often reduce verb forms. You may hear people say a sentence like "I gotta go." This is acceptable in informal speaking, but grammatically incorrect and inappropriate in writing. Compare the spoken and written statements below. Be careful not to use reduced verbs in your writing.

Spoken	Written
You better hurry.	You had better hurry.
I been working.	I've been working.
I'm gonna go.	I'm going to go.
I wanna watch TV.	I want to watch TV.
I gotta go.	I've got to go.

Revising

PEER REVISING

Exchange your Writing Assignment 2 paper about your important decision (page 60) with a partner. Focus on the questions on the Writing Checklist, below.

> ### Writing Checklist
>
> 1. Does the paragraph contain a topic sentence with a controlling idea?
> 2. Do the ideas in the paragraph actually follow the controlling idea in the topic sentence?
> 3. Do the ideas in the paragraph flow smoothly?
> 4. Are transitional words or phrases used to show the relations between ideas?
> 5. Are enough details given to make the major points clear?
> 6. Is there a conclusion?

Using your partner's suggestions, revise your paragraph as necessary.

EDITING VERBS

Choosing the appropriate verb tenses and forming verbs correctly are constant problems for learners of English. In writing, especially, you must be more attentive to using verbs correctly, since writing is a more formal type of communication than speaking.

To take an active role in controlling your verb usage, start by becoming a careful self-editor. Always reread your writing after you write the first draft, or first version. Self-editing is best done by focusing on one particular grammatical or mechanical problem area at a time. If you simply read your writing for ''errors'' in general, you will often miss some!

Begin this practice by focusing on verbs. After you have made the changes in content and organization that your partner suggested, read your paragraph once more, concentrating only on verbs. Find the verbs you have used. Check the tenses and the forms of the verbs and make appropriate changes.

Journal Writing

A. Write an answer to one of the questions below in your journal:

1. When you look back on a past decision, do you think you made the right choice?

2. Write about a bad decision you made. What were the consequences?

B. Write a one- or two-page entry on a topic of your choice.

More Writing Topics

1. Write a paragraph about a friend or a family member who made an important decision.

2. Write a paragraph about one effect of a decision you made.

3. Write a paragraph about a time you made a decision that was unpopular with others.

Chapter 4

The
Importance
of Place

What is a favorite place for you now?

What makes this place special?

Is there a special place that you remember from your past? Why is it special to you?

A Special Place

Getting Ideas

PHOTOGRAPHS

1

_____

_____

2

_____

_____

3   4

_____   _____

_____   _____

Discussion   In a group, examine the photographs on page 68 and above and briefly answer these questions about each of them.

1. What is the most important or the most striking thing in the picture?
   Write a word or two next to each photograph to describe the most important part.

2. How does the photograph make you feel? Which parts of the picture give you this feeling? Why? Write a word or two next to each photograph.

Composing

DESCRIPTIVE PARAGRAPH: TOPIC SENTENCE

When you describe a place, you need a particular kind of topic sentence. Simply introducing the place or telling where it is located is not enough; your topic sentence should say something interesting and important about the place.

Look at the two possible topic sentences below:

> **My bedroom is my favorite place.**
> **My bedroom is a refuge from all the stress in my life.**

Do the two topic sentences include both a topic and a controlling idea? Which one is more interesting? Why?

Clearly, the second sentence is more appealing because it says something interesting and important about the topic. It makes the reader want to know about the place and why this place feels like a refuge.

In your description of a special place, you should begin with a topic sentence that says something about the place that will invite someone to read your paragraph. For this assignment, the topic will be your special place, and the controlling idea will be what you say about the place.

Exercise 4.1   Use the photographs on pages 68 and 69. Write one sentence about each photograph that says something interesting and important about the place.

> *Example*   **Photograph on page 67**
>
> *This scene of a busy street in New York City gives me a feeling of excitement.*
>
> (This sentence describes the place and tells how it makes you feel.)
>
> or
>
> *The street in New York is bustling with activity.*
> (This sentence tells what kind of place it is.)

1. Photo 1: _____

   _____

2. Photo 2: _____

   _____

3. Photo 3: _____

   _____

4. Photo 4: _____

   _____

DESCRIPTIVE PARAGRAPH: SUPPORTING SENTENCES

To describe places like those in the photographs on pages 67-69, a writer should include many supporting details. In descriptive writing, the support is the writer's description of the sights, sounds, feelings, and smells of the place. These descriptive details enable the reader to clearly "see," "hear," "feel," or "smell" the place. The more specific the details are, the easier it is for the reader to experience the place.

Look at these two sentences:

> **Seagulls fly in the sky.**
>
> **Grey seagulls fly gracefully in the red and orange sky.**

Which sentence do you like better? Why?

The second sentence is a better supporting sentence for a descriptive paragraph because it contains specific details, the "grey seagulls" and "the red and orange sky." Also, "gracefully" tells how the seagulls fly. These help "paint a picture" of the place in the mind of the reader.

Exercise 4.2 To practice writing descriptive supporting sentences, write two sentences each for the photograph on pages 68 and 69. What do you see, hear, smell, feel? Your sentences should express sensory details.

> *Examples*   Photograph on page 67
>
> *Taxis, cars, and buses crowd the city street.*
>
> or
>
> *It is hard to cross the street because of all the traffic.*

PARAGRAPH ANALYSIS

Read this descriptive paragraph and then, with your group, answer the questions below.

My Thoughts in a Relaxing Place

When I need to be alone to think, the best place for me is the sea. At the ocean, there is no sound from people; all is calm. There is only the murmur of the waves bumping against the rocky coast. I like to walk on the beach especially when the sun goes down behind the horizon, and the sea begins to turn into red. I see the fishing boats with their large nets in the middle of the immense sea. Above, the grey seagulls fly in the red and orange sky. Sometimes they swoop down, picking up tiny food from the surrounding mountains. On the coast, the shells reflect many different bright colors: blue, orange, yellow, and violet. It seems to be like a little rainbow rising from the water. On the beach, the blue crabs run fast, trying to catch up with the waves. When I walk on the beach, my feet slide slowly in the fresh sand. Then, sitting on the wet rocks, I feel the breeze of the wind crossing my body. The strong waves dampen my bare legs. At this time, the breeze begins to be cool. I contemplate the landscape. I begin to think.

> *Irma Portillo*
> *Mexico*

Discussion:

1. What is the topic sentence of this paragraph?

2. Identify the senses that are described in the paragraph.

3. Do all the supporting sentences relate to the topic sentence?

4. Does the ordering of the supporting sentences seem logical?

A SPECIAL PLACE: TOPIC SENTENCE AND SUPPORT

Exercise 4.3 Think of your own special place. It might be a place you visited in the past or a place you visit now. Write a topic sentence that presents the place and says something interesting or important about it. Your topic sentence might introduce these ideas: how the place makes you feel, what kind of place it is, or the thing you like most about it.

Then, write three or four sentences that show some of the sensory experiences you have in this place (what you "hear," "feel," "smell," or "see").

Example topic sentences: **The abandoned farmhouse reminds me of childhood summers at my uncle's farm.**

As I sip coffee at a sidewalk café in Paris, I become energized by the sights and sounds around me.

Topic Sentence: _____

_____

_____

Supporting Sentences:

1. _____

2. _____

3. _____

4. _____

Writing

Using the ideas that you generated in Exercise 4.3, write one paragraph about your special place. Begin with the topic sentence you wrote for Exercise 4.3 that presents the place and tells something interesting or important about it.

Make sure all the supporting sentences relate to the topic sentence. Use specific details to express your sensory experiences at the place. As you write, consider your audience. Remember that your readers do not have a visual image and will be relying on you to paint the picture with words.

SENTENCE PATTERNS: THERE IS/THERE ARE

The writer of "My Thoughts in a Relaxing Place" uses several different sentence patterns to describe the beach. Two of these patterns were presented in chapter 1. The first is the Who or What Does What? pattern. In these sentences, the subject is the doer of the action in the verb. The second pattern is the Subject + Linking Verb + Complement type. Here, the subject does not do anything; rather, it is linked with a complement.

Reread these two sentences, which were taken from "My Thoughts in a Relaxing Place":

Example **On the coast, the shells reflect many different bright colors: blue, orange, yellow, and violet. It seems to be like a little rainbow rising from the water.**

Which sentence pattern does each sentence follow?

Example

What	Does What?
The shells	**reflect . . . colors**

What +	Linking Verb + Complement
It	**seems** **to be like a little rainbow rising from the water**

Examine this passage:

At the sea, there is no sound from people; all is calm. There is only the murmur of the waves bumping against the rocky coast. I like to walk on the beach especially when the sun goes down behind the horizon, and the sea begins to turn into red. I see the fishing boats with their large nets in the middle of the immense sea.

The first two sentences of the passage employ another common sentence pattern in English: There Is/There Are. Here, the word *there* is a false subject: it is not the doer of the action. This pattern expresses the existence of a subject that follows *There is* or *There are*. The verb *be* must agree with the subject that follows it.

Notice the pattern of these sentences:

There is/are +	Noun + (Subject)	Optional: adverb phrase of place or time adjective phrase

Noun   Adverb phrase of place

Examples **There are two large flowerpots on the windowsill.**

Noun   Adjective phrase

There is a globe lamp shedding light on the flowerpots.

There Is/There Are sentences are useful in description; however, note that the student writer of "My Thoughts in a Relaxing Place" does not overuse this pattern. Instead, she uses it in combination with Who Does What? and other types of sentence patterns.

Can you write the two example There Is/There Are sentences on the bottom of page 73, using another sentence pattern?

1. _____

2. _____

Exercise 4.4   With a partner, scan your classroom. Select three features of the room that you wish to describe, and write two sentences for each feature. Make one of the sentences follow the There Is/There Are pattern and the other sentence describe the same part of the classroom using another sentence pattern.

     Examples   *There is a large world map on the back wall.*
                    A large map of the world hangs on the back wall.

1. _____

_____

2. _____

_____

3. _____

_____

SUBJECT-VERB AGREEMENT

The simple present tense is commonly used to describe a place.

Look at these descriptive sentences:

        In the spring, wildflowers cover the field in front of the farmhouse.
        A small creek runs near the house.

Find the subject and verb of each sentence. How does the subject-verb of the first sentence differ from the subject-verb of the second sentence?

The subject of the first sentence, *wildflowers,* is plural, so the plural verb form *cover* is used. In the second sentence the singular *he-she-it* subject, *creek,* takes a singular verb with an *-s* ending: *runs.*

Both of the sentences above are grammatically correct because their subjects and verbs agree in number. Subject-verb agreement can prove troublesome in sentences with the following features:

1. The subject is followed by a descriptive phrase.

     Example   **The flowers in the field are blue, yellow, and red.**

2. The subject is a noncount noun.

   Example   **The fruit looks good enough to eat.**

3. The subject is an irregular plural noun.

   Example   **Many black catfish swim in the creek.**

4. The sentence has two subjects.

   Example   **A rake and a shovel rest against the side of the barn.**

5. The sentence begins with *There is* or *There are.*

   Example   **There are two metal chairs in the front yard.**

Exercise 4.5   With a partner or by yourself, edit the paragraph below for errors in subject-verb agreement. Begin by finding the main subject and verb of each sentence. Change the verb if it does not agree in number with the subject. Some sentences contain no errors. Correct the errors above each line.

A Spring Day at Leo's Farm

My friend Leo's farm in rural Texas is a peaceful place to spend a spring afternoon. A dirt road lead to the main gate of the farm. All the names of Leo's family appear on a sign above the gate. As I walk through the gate, I see a field of beautiful wildflowers. Bluebonnets and red "Indian paint brushes" lines both sides of the road. The bright red farmhouse stand beyond the field. In front of the house, two small tree swings invites the children to play. On lazy days, I join Leo on a wooden porch swing to catch up on the news from the small town where he lives. An older farmhouse to the left catch my eye. It reminds me of the times I spent there as a child and of the many times Leo whistled at me and the other children to bring him a hammer or boards as he built the new, red farmhouse. Behind both structures, there are an old barn with many treasures, but today I feel drowsy from the afternoon sun, so I leave them for another day. The wind blow through the trees as I walk to the garden nearby. Fruit ripen on the peach and apricot trees. The wild shrubs and flowers adds an exotic aroma to the air, attracting bees and other insects. Leo beckons me to the pond behind the garden, where his wood ducks and turkeys lives. Nearby, wild birds calls each other in the thick woods. Later, I will take a long walk in the forest, but, for the moment, the farm is enough. It make me feel so content and peaceful that I lie down in the grass to savor its sights and sounds.

Exercise 4.6   With a partner, write descriptive sentences in the simple present tense for the subjects below. Make sure that the verbs agree in number with the subjects.

Example   **ducks in the pond**
The ducks in the pond flap their wings when they get excited.

1. shells on the beach

2. people in the street

3. a cat and a dog

4. the water

5. a young man

VOCABULARY: USING DESCRIPTIVE WORDS

One challenge of writing is to find just the right words to express the ideas that you have in mind. Descriptive writing, in particular, requires the writer to choose vivid and meaningful descriptors—words that make the description come alive.

Without these descriptors, the "painting" that you create of a place lacks color and detail. The reader cannot experience the place as you see it. Thus, it is important to include vivid descriptive words that help the reader "see," "hear," "smell," and "feel" the place.

In the second sentence, descriptors help a reader experience the place more clearly.

At night, people walk around the town square of Mérida, Mexico.

Expanded: **At night, many people walk slowly around the well-lit town square of Mérida, Mexico.**

Exercise 4.7   Add descriptive details before or after the underlined words in the following paragraph. One sentence has been expanded as an example.

Example   **It's a place to have an enjoyable day.**
It's a pleasant place to have an enjoyable and restful day.

My Father's Backyard

My favorite place is my father's backyard. It's located in northern Puerto Rico in the mountains, far away from the city. It's a place to have an enjoyable day. Waking up in the morning before the sun rises, I can see all the city wake up. The chickens, their chicks and a chorus of roosters say, "Wake up!" or "Good morning!" The cow and her calf, a hawk looking for snacks, and all the other wonders of nature are there. Maybe I cannot visit it every day, but I like that place a lot. When I feel sad, I think about my time there and I feel happy.

Evelyn Chinea
Puerto Rico

VOCABULARY: FINDING SYNONYMOUS PHRASES

Another challenge in descriptive writing is not to fall into the habit of using the same descriptors over and again, describing a landscape as *beautiful*, or telling how you *walk by* the ocean, or *see* a sunset. The writer must increase his or her bank of words by exploring synonyms in a dictionary or thesaurus. The first step is to be aware that writing involves expanding your use of language and finding new and fresh ways to express ideas.

Practice enlarging your word bank by doing the following exercise. Then, try to use new words in your own writing.

Exercise 4.8   With a partner, find as many synonymous phrases as possible for the words underlined below. Brainstorm for synonyms together; then use a dictionary or thesaurus if necessary.

1. walk along the beach
2. see a bird in the sky
3. a large room
4. a beautiful sunrise
5. enjoy the place
6. a good experience
7. a hot summer day
8. I like the mountains
9. an advantage of living alone
10. a nice day

VOCABULARY: PREPOSITIONS OF PLACE

Look at this passage from the paragraph "My Thoughts in a Relaxing Place," which contains prepositions.

> **I see the fishing boats with their large nets in the middle of the immense sea. Above, the grey seagulls fly in the red and orange sky.**

Which prepositions indicate place? Which do not?

Exercise 4.9   Scan "A Spring Day at Leo's Farm" on page 75 to find prepositions that show place location or direction. Circle each place preposition, and make a list of them below.

_____   _____   _____

_____   _____   _____

_____   _____   _____

_____   _____   _____

Exercise 4.10   With a partner, fill in the blanks of the following paragraph with an appropriate preposition of place location or direction. For several blanks, there is more than one possibility.

My City Retreat

The creek _____ my neighborhood _____ Philadelphia lies deep _____ the woods, serving as a peaceful retreat from the city. The woods emerge _____ the end _____ a dead-end street. The creek is located _____ the woods. Suddenly, tall trees and thick bushes replace the houses and concrete. _____ a street lamp, the trees stand upright like an army of nature's soldiers battling the intrusion of the city. The moment I step _____ the woods, I enter another world. Walking cautiously _____ the creek, I hear tree branches creak and leaves rustle. I feel certain that the animals _____ the woods are watching me. _____ the creek, the water runs lazily _____ the rocks, gurgling at me invitingly. I dunk my feet _____ the cool water, and I feel the smoothness of the rocks _____ my feet. The city feels far away. Sitting _____ the black clay banks, I savor the solitude of this place. I am happy when no one intrudes on my quiet moments here. In early evening, the woods grow dark and cool. I can sense the animals moving _____ me. The wind begins to blow the trees and bushes, and birds signal that night is coming. I am scared, but, nevertheless, I do not leave. Then, night falls too quickly, and I must return _____ my city life.

SENTENCE PATTERNS: PARTICIPIAL PHRASE + MAIN CLAUSE

Look at this sentence from "My Thoughts in a Relaxing Place":

> **Sitting on the wet rocks, I feel the breeze of the wind crossing my body.**

Who feels the breeze? Who is sitting on the wet rocks? What is another way to say this?

The *-ing* phrase at the beginning of this sentence is a participial phrase. A participial phrase is a reduction of a dependent clause. In the sentence above, the two actions, of sitting and feeling, are done by the same person and occur at the same time. The same idea could be expressed in another way:

> **While *I* am sitting on the wet rocks, *I* feel the breeze of the wind crossing my body.**

The writer can reduce the dependent clause to a phrase because the subjects of the main and dependent clauses are the same. In order to reduce a dependent time clause, follow these steps:

1. Omit the time word *when, while,* or *as.*

2. Omit the subject.

3. If there is a form of the verb *be,* omit it.

4. If there is no form of the verb *be,* change the verb to the *-ing* form.

Look at these examples:

> **While I am walking down the path, I am overwhelmed by the sweet fragrance of flowers.**

> **Walking down the path, I am overwhelmed by the sweet fragrance of flowers.**

> **As the waves crash onto the rocks, they produce a fine salty spray.**
> **Crashing onto the rocks, the waves produce a fine salty spray.**

Note that when the time clause is reduced, the noun subject (the waves) is put in the main clause.

Now examine this sentence:

> **While the white ducks flew over my head, I stopped my car to watch them.**

Can you reduce the dependent time clause to a phrase in that sentence?

In that sentence, the time of the two actions is the same; however, the sentence cannot be reduced because the subjects of the two clauses are different.

Notice the error that results when you reduce a clause with a different subject:

> **Flying over my head, I stopped to watch them.**

That sentence means "I was flying over my head," which is clearly impossible.

Exercise 4.11   Reduce the sentences below when possible by making one of the clauses a participial phrase. Mark the sentences "Not possible" if the sentences cannot be reduced.

1. When I watch the waves, I feel calm.

2. When I see a young boy with his father, I think about my childhood.

3. While the boat is floating down the river, it makes ripples in the water.

4. As I wander into the room, a friendly man named Eric walks across to us.

5. As the sun rises over the valley, it spreads its golden glow.

Exercise 4.12   Expand the participial phrases into clauses in the sentences below.

1. Flying onto a branch, the bluebird begins to sing.

2. Reading a book in the park, I savor the sunshine on my back.

3. Thinking deeply, I was startled when my friend said "hello."

4. Looking out the window, the children wait for their playmate to arrive.

5. Approaching the river, I feel a coolness in the air.

Revising

Exchange papers about your special place (Writing Assignment, page 72) with a partner. Answer these Writing Checklist questions.

Writing Checklist

1. Does the topic sentence say something important or interesting about the place?

2. Do the ideas in the paragraph support the topic sentence?

3. Are descriptive words used?

4. Do the details express the sights, sounds, smells, and feelings of the place, giving you a clear picture of it?

5. Do all the subjects and verbs agree?

Now, using the information your partner has given you, revise your paragraph.

WRITING ASSIGNMENT 2

A Center of Activity

Getting Ideas

CHOOSING A TOPIC

For this writing assignment, you and a partner will visit a center of activity at your educational institution and take notes about what you see, smell, hear, and feel; then, each of you will write a paragraph about the place.

Begin by discussing with your partner which center of activity on campus interests you. Choose a place that has a lot of activity, with students or employees, teachers or visitors. A place with visual variety or a clear function may also be good choices.

When you have chosen a center of activity, first be prepared to open your senses to the place. At the center of activity, find a comfortable place from which you can take thorough notes about what you see, hear, smell, and feel. Using descriptive words, write down as many details as you can. If you have questions about the vocabulary of any parts of the place, be ready to ask them in class, but write down something that will help you remember the unknown words.

BRAINSTORMING

After you have visited your center of activity, discuss with your partner the impression, or feeling, that you both got from the place. In the blanks below, write adjectives that describe your dominant impression, or main feeling, of the place. The "dominant impression" may relate how the place makes you feel, the general activity of the place, or the general appearance of the place.

_____

_____

_____

Now, write one adjective that relates your overall impression of the place:

_____

Look at your notes from Choosing a Topic again. Circle the details that relate to the word above. Do most of your details relate to this word? If so, this may be a good word to keep in mind when you write your topic sentence and paragraph. If not, brainstorm another adjective to express your dominant impression.

Composing

A CENTER OF ACTIVITY: TOPIC SENTENCE

The topic sentence of this descriptive composition should introduce the place and say something about it. For this writing assignment, the topic is the center of activity, and the controlling idea tells the writer's dominant impression of the place.

Examples **The bookstore is so crowded and disorganized that it makes me feel claustrophobic.**

The cafeteria is the heart of the university, since many students meet there throughout the day to study and socialize.

Write a tentative topic sentence for your center of activity in the blanks below. (Since your ideas and your partner's may differ, you will each write a separate paragraph.)

_____

_____

_____

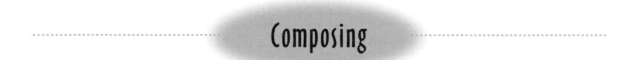

Getting Ideas

FREEWRITING

- Using your tentative topic sentence about a center of activity, think of details that will best focus on this main idea.
- Write for three minutes about the center of activity, starting with the topic sentence.
- When you have finished, reread what you have written. Cross out sentences that do not relate to the topic sentence.
- Then, continue writing where you left off, and write for another three minutes.
- Read over what you have written to find ideas that relate to your topic sentence.

If your freewriting sends you in another direction, revise your topic sentence accordingly.

Composing

COHERENCE: ORDERING OF DETAILS IN DESCRIPTION

Look again at the photographs at the beginning of the chapter. The way you might "paint" these pictures with words depends on the content of each photograph and on your own perspective. The way you order the supporting details will, therefore, be unique. However, the sequence should follow some logical order.

- One way to arrange the details is by describing a place in spatial order: you first describe one area of the place, then move to a second area and describe it, and so forth. Most important, you should not jump back and forth, first describing one section of a place, then a second section, and then returning to the first section.
- Another way is to begin with an outstanding or unusual element that attracts you, using order of importance.

Be sure that your description of a place is arranged in a particular logical sequence of details. Let the place and the main idea of your description (what you say about the place) determine your arrangement.

Exercise 4.12 Reread "My Thoughts in a Relaxing Place," on page 71. With a partner, discuss which type of sequencing of details the writer uses: describing a place by spatial order or by order of importance.

Exercise 4.13 Read the following descriptive paragraph, paying special attention to the logical sequence of details. In a group, answer the questions that follow.

A Place to Awaken Your Senses

There is a wonderful, quiet site on my hometown river. Every summer this site becomes my favorite place. It is located near my house, and you can get to it by going down a winding footpath. I used to go there in the afternoons before sunset, when the heat was finally bearable. As you begin to go down, the cool breeze welcomes you and invites you to enjoy the stillness of the place. First, you can see the tall green trees between whose branches you can have a glimpse of a broken mirror. Near the river bank, the smoothness of the grass makes your shoes feel uncomfortable and makes you anxiously bare your feet. Lying down under the fresh shade, you can hear the wind whispering—trying to convince the leaves to share its game—and birds singing, perhaps laughing at the strange colloquy. The weeping willows stretch down their languid branches to touch the water, as though wanting to absorb the last sunlight reflected on the surface. The mix of fragrances of the grass, wild flowers, and humid ground makes a ticklish, bittersweet aroma. Soon, the first star appears in the horizon, announcing the coming of night. It is time to leave, but your spirit has retained the beauty of a summer afternoon. When I go to my hometown every summer, I visit this place, but if I can't go, I resort to my memories and recover the serenity that I find in this place.

Jesus Aguirre
Mexico

Discussion:

1. How is the description of the parts of this place ordered—by spatial order, or by order of importance? Is this order logical?

2. If the paragraph is arranged by order of importance, what is the most important element? If spatial order is used, in what direction is the place described?

3. Which connecting words does the writer use to show the relation between the parts in the place?

4. Do you like the description? Why?

PARAGRAPH UNITY: FOCUSED DESCRIPTION

Look around your classroom. Imagine that you wanted to describe this room to someone and express your dominant impression—that the room made you feel uncomfortable. Which elements of the room would support this main idea? Which elements would not relate to the idea that the room is uncomfortable?

If you said that your classroom was uncomfortable because the chairs were hard and the lighting was poor, these supporting details would relate to the main idea. However, if you simply stated that the room had four windows, how would that detail relate to "uncomfortable"? Could you include this information in a way that would relate it to the main idea?

A writer could use the windows of a room to support the main idea that the room is uncomfortable like this:

> **The four small windows in the room are clouded over by layers of dirt and grease.**

That sentence contributes to the idea that the room is uncomfortable.

When you describe a place, it is not necessary to describe everything in the place. Instead, focus on the main idea expressed in the topic sentence. Think about what you wish to relate to the reader about the place. Then, select only those descriptive details that convey this idea.

Exercise 4.14 Read the following student paragraphs below. Cross out any supporting details that do not relate to the topic sentence.

My Bedroom

My bedroom is dark and cramped. The moment you enter the front door, your eyes are drawn to the black and brown furniture. On the left wall, a large black chest of drawers rests near the door. Its drawers are overfilled, and clothes often spill out onto the floor. On the adjacent wall, my dark wooden desk, cluttered with papers, is crammed tightly between two black bookcases. It's relaxing to sit here and write letters or do my homework. There is a small window behind the desk, but it is hidden by the desk, and the dark blue curtains block out all the sunlight. Books and papers in the bookcases lie in disorganized stacks. My black iron bunk bed, which rests against the back wall of the room, is covered with a dark blue bedspread that also darkens the room. I bought the bunk bed because I had always wanted one as a child. The top bunk of the bed is covered with more debris—books, tapes, papers, drink cups—all of which makes me feel the whole room is overloaded with furniture and possessions. Under the bed are more belongings that add to my feeling of claustrophobia. Beside my bed is a small black bookcase with a light, and stacks of pictures, cards, and other possessions that I have not found time to organize. The overall feeling I get from my room is that it is overcrowded and oppressive. I hate to say it, but I enjoy my bedroom the most when I am not there.

Walking on the Beach of the North Sea

I like to walk on the wet sand of the North Sea beach in the wintertime. Probably, you have never seen a picture of that because people prefer to spend a vacation in a place with blue sky and green sea. There, it is different. It's the winter, with a lot of wind. Every day it's rainy, cloudy, and foggy. I love to walk in the rain in the city, too. The first reaction for a normal person if you see this weather is to stay at home in comfort. However, I like to walk for hours here with a big coat and my dog. I feel good, refreshed and healthy. At this moment, I feel my body is alive. I think about everything. Sometimes, I see the figure of somebody, or maybe it's a dream. I hear the noise of the waves, the howl of the wind, and the cry of the seagulls. They like to make fun of me. Sometimes, I keep old bread and I throw it at the birds. The wind brings the sea smell, the smell of seaweed or shellfish. The beach is also pleasant in the springtime, but it is less cold and windy. With each step, I leave my footprints in the sand, the proof of my passage in case I disappear in the fog. On one side of the beach, I see the sea in fury, and on the other side, the dunes. When I am in the dunes, it is less windy. It is a strange spectacle in this place. Time stopped in 1945. At the beginning of World War II, the German army built big bunkers to protect the port, and they are still there. Children like to play "war" on this construction. I like this place, not only the beach or the dunes, but everything because when I feel sad, tired, or just want to think about my life, my friends, or things to be done, it's the best place for me. I think it's because sometimes I feel like I want to fly with the sea birds.

Denis Vandenbosch
Belgium

COHERENCE: USING REFERENCE WORDS

In chapter 3, you learned two important ways to achieve coherence in your writing: ordering ideas logically and using transition words. In this chapter, you have examined how to add coherence to descriptive writing by ordering details logically. Yet another way to make your writing smoother is by using appropriate reference items. These words or phrases enable the writer to refer to something mentioned earlier without repeating the same word or words.

For example, look at this sentence:

I can't follow the fashion because it is designed for slim people.

Here, the pronoun *it* refers to the fashion. If the writer repeated the word *fashion,* the sentence would be awkward.

Look at another sentence:

When I think of my parents, I feel bad because I didn't have a good relationship with my parents.

Can the sentence be improved?

The sentence is not smooth because the writer repeats the phrase *my parents* unnecessarily. It would be better to write the sentence like this:

When I think of my parents, I feel bad because I didn't have a good relationship with them.

Reference words are very important tools for tying a piece of writing together. However, you must be sure to use them correctly. In this chapter, you will practice using pronouns in place of nouns or phrases. For a review of the kinds of pronouns there are in English, refer to your grammar book or consult with your teacher.

Exercise 4.15 Read the following sentences. If possible, eliminate unnecessary repetition by using appropriate pronouns.

Rewrite each sentence on a separate piece of paper.

    Example 1:   **My teacher advised me to apply to graduate school, and my teacher wrote me a letter of recommendation.**

    Better: **My teacher advised me to apply to graduate school, and he wrote me a letter of recommendation.**

    Example 2:   **Kenting National Park is the most popular tourist attraction in Taiwan. When you go to Kenting National Park, you will find beautiful birds and exotic plants.**

    Better: **Kenting National Park is the most popular tourist attraction in Taiwan. When you go there, you will find beautiful birds and exotic plants.**

1. If I borrow a car from my friend, I should drive his car carefully, and before I return the car, I should fill the car with gasoline.

2. When I don't understand what a teacher is saying, I should raise my hand and ask the teacher to explain immediately.

3. I needed a car, but before I could buy a car, I had to save enough money.

4. We had planned to visit the museum, but when we got to the museum, it was closed.

5. In the past, people had to go shopping in stores that were far from one another. People wasted time and gasoline going from one store to another, but now people have shopping centers.

6. My sister spent all her money on a guitar, but spending all of her money on a guitar was a waste because she never learned how to play the guitar.

7. When the Chinese are in a class or office, the Chinese don't usually say too much.

COHERENCE: PRONOUN CONSISTENCY

When using a pronoun, you must be sure that it is consistent or agrees with the noun it refers to. Look at these sentences:

1. People who don't budget **their** money often find **they** cannot pay all **their** bills.

2. People who don't budget **his** money often find **he** cannot pay all **his** bills.

In the first sentence, the plural pronouns *their, they* and *their* all correctly refer to the plural noun *People*.

In the second, the singular pronouns *his, he* and *his* are not consistent with the plural noun *People*.

Exercise 4.16   Each sentence has an error or errors in pronoun consistency. Correct any errors you find in use of pronouns and related nouns and verbs. Make corrections above each line.

    Example   **If we want to make our lives better, ~~you~~ must never stop learning.** [we]

1. The food that we had at the restaurant was excellent, but they were expensive.

2. A person should take care of their health.

3. A doctor should be allowed to help all patients and save his life.

4. Working women have hard lives. She has to get up early in the morning and help her family get ready.

5. After a short time, the drug user can be satisfied only with the drug. They will do anything to get the drug.

6. Americans love shopping malls. They like to go to malls because you can do all your shopping in one place.

7. There are obvious differences between men and women. No one can change it.

8. It's important for the engineer to know a second language, especially when they work for an oil company.

Writing

Use your notes and the skills you have gained to write a paragraph about the center of activity on campus that you have chosen. Be sure that your paragraph has a topic sentence that focuses on your dominant impression of the place and that includes specific details to support this focus. Also, add a concluding sentence. Remember that your audience may not be familiar with the scene, so you should make the center of activity come alive for the readers.

When you have finished, give your paragraph an interesting title.

Building Language Skills

RUN-ON SENTENCES

Read this sentence aloud:

> **To get a passport in Taiwan, you must first take your ID and five hundred N.T. dollars to the government passport office when you get there, you should fill out an application form.**

As you read the sentence, where do you naturally pause?

You probably paused after *office*, because that is where the first sentence should end. A second sentence begins with "When you get . . .".

These sentences are not correctly written. We call the mistake in them a *run-on sentence* because there are two complete sentences (independent clauses) with no punctuation or connecting words between them.

To correct a run-on sentence, you can do the following (note the added punctuation and words are underscored):

1. Put a period or semicolon between the two independent clauses.

   To get a passport in Taiwan, you must first take your ID and five hundred N.T. dollars to the government passport office. When you get there, you should fill out an application form.

2. Use a comma and a coordinating conjunction between the two independent clauses.

   To get a passport in Taiwan, you must first take your ID and five hundred N.T. dollars to the government passport office, and when you get there, you should fill out an application form.

3. Use a subordinating conjunction.

   You fill out the application form you return it to the clerk. (run-on sentence)
   After you fill out the application form, you return it to the clerk.

In English, two independent clauses must be separated by a period or a semicolon, or they must be connected with a coordinator or subordinator.

COMMA-SPLICE SENTENCES

Note that simply placing a comma between the two clauses does not correct a run-on sentence. This, in fact, is a related mistake—*a comma-splice error.*

Read this sentence:

He speaks English with a strange accent, it is hard to understand everything he says.

You can correct a comma-splice error in the same way that you correct a run-on sentence:

1. Put a period or semicolon between the independent clauses.

   He speaks English with a strange accent; it is hard to understand everything he says.

2. Use a comma and a coordinator.

   He speaks English with a strange accent, so it is hard to understand everything he says.

3. Use a subordinator.

   Because he speaks English with a strange accent, it is hard to understand everything he says.

You are likely to make a comma-splice error when you use transitional expressions.

New Orleans has many wonderful places of entertainment, for example, there are hundreds of nightclubs with music and dancing.

To correct that sentence, put a semicolon or a period before *for example.*

Exercise 4.17 Identify and correct the run-on sentences or comma-splice errors in the following groups of words. You may add correct punctuation or connecting words. Some of the sentences may be correct as written. Rewrite each sentence on a separate piece of paper.

1. Learning a language takes a lot of time, some people spend years studying before they can speak a second language well.

2. When we arrived at the campsite, we tried to set up the tent unfortunately it was too windy and we couldn't get it to stay up.

3. When you plan a party, you should first make a list of people you want to invite, then decide what kind of food you will serve.

4. Although the sun was shining brightly, the cold wind stung our faces and brought tears to our eyes.

5. I decided to become an astronomer because I have always loved the stars and planets I hope I can get into an astronomy program.

6. Many people spend a lot of time and money on health clubs, however, they continue to eat unhealthy foods.

Revising

Reread the paragraph you wrote about a center of activity, (Writing Assignment 2, page 87) focusing on the following Writing Checklist questions; then, revise your composition.

Writing Checklist

1. Does the paragraph have a main-idea sentence that focuses on the writer's dominant impression of the place?

2. Do all the ideas in the paragraph support this dominant impression?

3. Are descriptive words and phrases used to strengthen the dominant impression?

4. Do all pronouns have clear referents?

5. Does the paragraph contain run-on sentences or comma splices?

Journal Writing

A. Write a one-page journal entry about one of the following topics:

1. Imagine that you are living in the perfect place for you. This place can be real or imagined. Describe it.

2. Describe a place that you find unpleasant or uncomfortable. Tell why you dislike the place and what aspects of the place you do not like.

B. Write a one-page entry on a topic or topics of your choice.

More Writing Topics

1. Write a paragraph to describe a tourist attraction in your city or country.

2. Write a paragraph to describe a relaxing place in the city where you now live.

3. Write a paragraph to describe one home where you lived as a child.

Chapter 5

Looking Outward

What features do you like best about your city? Which features do you like least?

What qualities do you look for in a person?

Analyzing My City

Getting Ideas

BRAINSTORMING

In chapter 4, you explored the importance of place. With your group, think about the city or town you are living in. Brainstorm all the positives and negatives about it. Under the plus signs, write the positives, and under the negative signs, write the negatives. An example of each is provided for you.

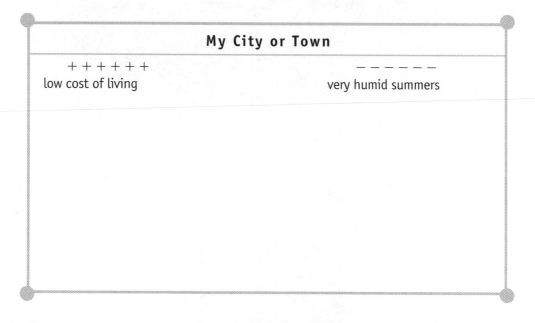

My City or Town

+ + + + + +

low cost of living

– – – – – –

very humid summers

GROUPING IDEAS

Now that you have gathered ideas about the city or town you live in, work with a partner to examine your ideas, and see if you can put them into groups. For example, if under negatives (disadvantages), you listed "very humid summers," "unpredictable temperatures," and "heavy rains," you could group these items together under the more general category, "weather."

Advantages	Disadvantages	
	Weather	unpredictable temperatures very humid summers heavy rains

Once you have finished, you should have a list of two to four general categories, each with two to four specific advantages (or disadvantages) under them.

Writing

Choose one of the following two topic sentences, and write a paragraph using the information you gathered in your brainstorming.

1. Living in (name of your city) has several advantages.

2. Living in (name of your city) has several disadvantages.

Composing

EXPANDING A PARAGRAPH INTO AN ESSAY

As you explore topics in greater depth, you will generate more ideas and will need to write compositions of more than one paragraph. For your next assignment, you will write a multi-paragraph essay.

What is an essay? An essay is simply an expanded discussion of a single topic. Just like a paragraph, an essay contains these parts:

- an introduction
- the body (support)
- a conclusion

However, in an essay each of these parts is expanded into a separate paragraph. In fact, in compositions about complicated subjects, the body usually takes several paragraphs.

Exercise 5.1   Read the paragraph below.

The Benefits of Living Alone

Living alone has several important advantages. First, you don't have to worry about making noise. You can play your music as loudly as you want. In addition, you can leave your things anywhere you want. You don't have to hang your clothes up. Finally, you have privacy. No one will interfere in your personal affairs. With these benefits, it is sometimes preferable to live by yourself.

The topic of this paragraph is <u>living alone</u>, and the controlling idea is <u>several important advantages</u>. The reader expects to find out what those advantages are.

Note that the writer has three major supporting points for the main idea:

1. You don't have to worry about making noise.

2. You can leave your things anywhere you want.

3. You have privacy.

These three points clearly support the central idea; however, they are not adequately developed. In other words, the writer has not included enough supporting detail to explain the major points.

Exercise 5.2   With a partner, think of more specific details that could be added to make each major supporting point stronger. Write one or two more sentences for each point.

1. You don't have to worry about making noise.
   You can play your music at full volume.

   _____

   _____

   _____

2. You can leave your things anywhere you want.
   You don't have to hang your clothes up.

   _____

   _____

   _____

3. You have privacy.
   No one will interfere in your personal affairs.

   _____

   _____

   _____

You could use your details to expand the paragraph into an essay. The reading below shows how one student did just that. Notice how each major supporting idea has become a complete body paragraph supported by detail.

READING: AN ESSAY EXPANDED FROM A PARAGRAPH
After you have finished reading the essay, answer the questions that follow with your classmates.

The Benefits of Living Alone

One of the most exciting events in a person's life is moving away from his or her family for the first time. Living alone is an important step toward independence and adulthood. With it come new responsibilities and freedoms. In fact, living alone has several important advantages.

First, when you live alone, you don't have to worry about how much noise you make. In the morning, you can wake up to loud music on the alarm radio. Then, when you are making coffee and toast, you don't have to be careful about dropping spoons or slamming cupboard doors. When you come home after school or work, you can listen to rock music on the stereo at full volume, or you can turn on the TV. You can even go to sleep with the stereo still on. No one will tell you to be quiet.

Another advantage of not having a roommate is that you can leave your things anywhere you want. You don't have to wash the dishes before you leave for work. You can even leave the butter and jam on the kitchen table instead of putting them back in the refrigerator. You can leave your dirty clothes wherever you take them off and pick them up when you decide to go to the laundromat. Books don't have to be put on the bookshelf and tapes don't have to be put away. You don't have to roll the tube of toothpaste or put the top back on. You can create your own chaos and no one will be disturbed.

Most important, when you live alone you have the benefit of having privacy. No one will interfere in your private affairs. No one will read your mail or listen to your phone calls to your lover. No one will listen to the messages on your answering machine and find out who is angry with you or who wants to see you. You can leave your letters out, you can put up pictures of special people, and you can walk around in your underwear. Your home is your private haven.

Many people argue that having a roommate is a big help, especially for foreign students living in the United States. Certainly there are some comforts in having a friend to live with, but there are also some pluses to living on your own. Having your own apartment means you can be noisy, be messy, and keep your privacy.

Discussion

1. What are the three main benefits of living alone? Find the sentences that express these three main advantages.

2. What details does the writer use to support these advantages?

THE PARTS OF AN ESSAY

Notice that the structure of an essay is similar to that of a paragraph. Compare the components of each:

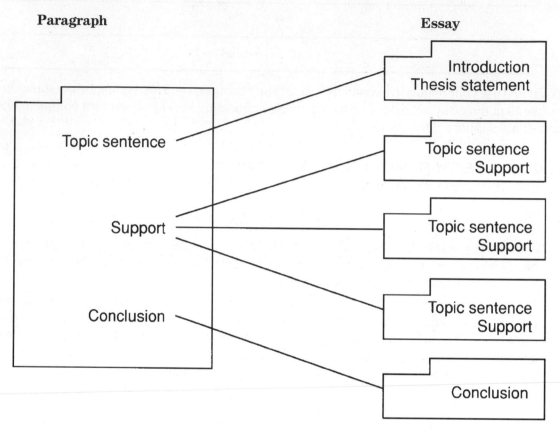

OUTLINING

Outlining is a way to organize writing. It helps you to keep in mind the order in which you will present your ideas. Experienced writers often use outlines as a way of keeping longer pieces of writing clearly organized, before and as they write.

Here is a sample outline for Writing Assignment 1.

I.   Introduction: Introduce the topic and present your thesis statement.
     Sample thesis statement: **Living in Philadelphia has several advantages.**

II. Body Paragraph 1: State the first major point in your topic sentence.

     Example topic sentence: **One advantage of living in Philadelphia is that there are many educational opportunities.**

     A.   Give a first supporting point.
     B.   Give a second supporting point.

III. Body paragraph 2: State the second major point in you topic sentence.

     A.   Give a first supporting point.
     B.   Give a second supporting point.

IV. Body paragraph 3: State the third major point in your topic sentence.
   A. Give first supporting point.
   B. Give a second supporting point.

V. Conclusion: Restate the thesis or your major points.

THE THESIS STATEMENT

In Chapters 1 and 2, you learned that the topic sentence expresses the main idea of the paragraph. The *thesis statement* expresses the main idea of the essay. Like the topic sentence, it controls or limits the piece of writing. The *thesis* differs from the topic sentence of a paragraph in that it encompasses the ideas in an entire essay, not just those in one paragraph.

The introductory paragraph of the essay can be represented as an inverted triangle: the broader, more general ideas about the topc lead to the narrower, more specific idea of the thesis statement.

Traditionally, the thesis statement appears at the end of the introductory paragraph, as the following diagram shows (Note: In some writing the thesis may be stated as the first sentence, in the middle of the introduction, or even in a later paragraph in longer pieces of writing):

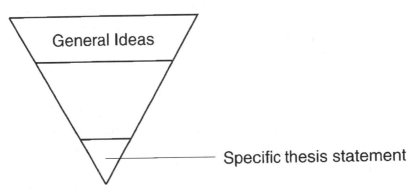

Go back to the essay "The Benefits of Living Alone," on pages 94-95. What is the thesis statement?

There are some important points to remember when writing your thesis statement:

1. A thesis statement must be a complete sentence.

   The advantages of San Francisco.   Not a thesis statement

   San Francisco is a city of many cultural attractions.   Thesis statement

2. A thesis statement is more interesting when it expresses an opinion or attitude about a topic rather than a statement of fact, which cannot be argued.

   New York City is the largest city in the United States.   Not a thesis statement

   New York City, the largest city in the United States, is a great place to live.   Thesis statement

3. A thesis statement is most often not a question.

   What are the advantages of having a roommate?   Not a thesis statement

   With a roommate, you have someone to share expenses, housework, and problems.   Thesis statement

4. A thesis statement may present more than one idea, but the ideas should be consistent.

Movies today show too much violence, and they use great special effects. — Not a thesis statement

In my opinion, movies today show too much violence. — Thesis statement

Exercise 5.3 Read the following groups of words and decide if each is a correct thesis statement or not. Try to change the incorrect phrases into correct thesis statements. Write any necessary revision under each sentence.

1. The dangers of mountain climbing.

2. My dog communicates with me in several ways.

3. There are many benefits to learning a second language, and it is difficult.

4. What are the characteristics of a good teacher?

5. A lot of violence on American television.

6. What makes television worth watching.

Exercise 5.4 In a group, brainstorm ideas for essays on the general topics below. On your own, write a thesis statement for each of the topics. Be sure that this sentence presents the topic and the controlling idea (what you want to say about the topic). Remember that the thesis statement must be a complete sentence. Write your thesis statements below each topic.

Example   **working while you are in college**
Having a part-time job while you are a college student can bring you several important benefits.

1. learning English

2. exercising

3. traveling alone

4. owning a car

5. being single

STARTING AN ESSAY

Look at these two models of an introductory paragraph. Find the thesis statement in each.

> Everyone tells us that exercise is good for our health. Newspapers, magazines, and television inform us that by exercising we can feel more energetic and even prolong our lives. We are encouraged to jog or swim, do aerobics, play tennis—any exercise that we find enjoyable. One form of exercise that I have discovered—walking—has some important benefits.

> When I was younger, I had many heroes. There was Superman, who battled against evil and always won. There were my brothers, who always wore the right clothes and said the right things. There was my seventh-grade math teacher, who could make fractions and algebraic equations easy to understand. There were the Beatles, who made the "most wonderful music in the world." Now that I am older, it is harder for me to identify a real hero, but the person I admire most is my friend Sam.

In both these introductions, the last sentence of the paragraph presents the thesis, or main idea. This statement tells the reader what to expect in the essay.

Notice how each introduction begins with general ideas about the topic that lead into what the writer wants to say about the topic—the thesis statement. In the first introduction, the general topic is the benefits of exercise. The author begins the introduction by giving some general information about the value of exercise; this leads into the thesis statement, which contains the controlling idea—that there are benefits to walking. In this essay, we expect to find out what those benefits are.

In the second introduction, the general topic is heroes, so the writer begins by mentioning some of her childhood heroes. She ends with the thesis statement, which expresses the controlling idea—that Sam is the person she most admires. In this essay, we expect to find out the reasons why Sam is the writer's hero.

PREPARING YOUR OWN OUTLINE

Before you write an essay about the advantages or disadvantages of living in your city or town, prepare a sentence outline to guide you. Refer to the sample outline on page 96.

Start by writing a thesis statement that expresses the main idea of your essay. The thesis statement will be included in Roman numeral I of your outline, the Introduction, as follows:

I.   Introduction
     Thesis Statement: _____

     _____

The next three parts of your outline will represent the body paragraphs: the major points of your essay, which, in this case, will be the advantages or disadvantages of living in your city.

Use Roman numerals to indicate paragraphs two through four of your essay. The example topic sentence on page 96 shows that the first sentence after each of the Roman numeral headings should be the topic sentence of that particular paragraph. Under each Roman numeral, use capital letters *A* and *B* to briefly state at least two supporting points to illustrate or ''prove'' the topic sentence. The supporting points should each be stated in phrases or sentences. (If you have more than two pieces of support, simply add point *C*, and so on.) Do the same with each of the Roman numerals that represent the body paragraphs.

For the conclusion, write one complete sentence that restates the thesis or your major points. When you have finished, work with a partner to review each other's outlines.

Writing

Use the outline you have just prepared, as well as your notes and the skills you have gained, to write a short essay in which you discuss the advantages or disadvantages of living in your city or town. Remember to name the city or town (and country if necessary) so that the audience will know where it is.

Revising

After you have written the first draft of your essay, have a partner read it and offer suggestions for revision. Have your partner consider the Writing Checklist questions below as he or she gives you advice.

Writing Checklist

1. Does the essay have an introductory paragraph? Does this paragraph begin with general ideas about the topic? Does it have a thesis statement?

2. Does each body paragraph have a topic sentence?

3. Do the topic sentences relate to the thesis statement?

4. Does the essay contain a concluding paragraph that restates the thesis statement and the major points of the essay?

5. In general, is the organization of the essay logical?

A Person I Admire

Getting Ideas

BRAINSTORMING

In a group, discuss these questions:

1. What is a hero? What does a hero do? What kinds of actions are heroic?

2. Who are your heroes?

3. Who do you admire? Why?

LISTING

Make a list of all the people in your life who have been important. Think about different aspects and areas of your life—family, school, friends, entertainment, and so on.

FREEWRITING

Pick one of the people you listed, and freewrite for ten minutes about this person. Tell why you admire him or her.

Remember that when you freewrite, you should not be concerned with grammar or spelling. Write quickly and without stopping about whatever comes to your mind.

Composing

SUPPORTING GENERALIZATIONS WITH EXAMPLES

When we write, we often make generalizations. A generalization is a statement about a person, place, thing, or idea that we believe is true in most cases. For example, the statement "The weather in San Diego is wonderful" is a general statement about the weather in San Diego.

In the next assignment, you are going to write about a personal hero or a person you admire. In writing this essay, you will also be making generalizations about this special person. For instance, *you* might say, "I admire Sam because he is honest."

When you make generalizations, you should support them with specific examples in order to prove or show that your statement is valid. The more detailed the examples, the more convincing your point will be. Usually, you will need from two to four representative examples to support a generalization.

Consider this statement: "I admire Sam because he is honest."

What kind of examples would best support this? You should think about different situations in which Sam has shown his honesty. Describe the situation and explain exactly what Sam does or doesn't do in that situation.

You might use examples such as these:

> **A. One day Sam and I went grocery shopping. Our purchases came to about $7.00, and Sam gave the cashier a $10.00 bill. She mistakenly gave him change for $20.00. Sam did not hesitate a moment. He immediately returned the extra money to the very grateful employee.**

(This example of Sam's honesty refers to a specific event in the past. For that reason, past tense verbs are used.)

> **B. If Sam hasn't done his homework and the teacher asks for a reason, he never invents an excuse, as most students do. He doesn't say that he left it at home or in his car. Sam simply tells the instructor that he didn't have time to do the assignment. He is direct and honest about what happened.**

(This example of Sam's truthfulness refers to his habitual actions, and in this case, present tense verbs are used.)

Exercise 5.5   For each of the following generalizations, write a supporting example below. Try to be as specific as possible. Use the appropriate verb tense.

1. My father guides me in the right direction.

2. (Name of person) is my hero because he enjoys life.

3. I respected my first English teacher because she was so patient.

ORDERING OF MAJOR POINTS

Just as supporting ideas in a paragraph should be logically ordered, the major points in an essay should be presented according to some principle of organization. The most basic ways they can be ordered are according to time, degree of familiarity, or level of importance.

When you wrote about the advantages or disadvantages of living in your city, you might have ordered the major points according to importance:

> **Order of importance: Start with the least important point and end with the most important.**

Or, you might have chosen to order the points according to familiarity:

> **Order of familiarity: Start with the most familiar point and end with the least familiar.**

When you use these two principles of organization, you should try to save the best for last.

If you were writing a story, as you did in chapter 2, you would, of course, order your ideas according to time. This is called chronological ordering.

      Order of time: **Start with the first event and end with the last.**

Think about your next assignment—writing about a hero or a person you admire. What would be the best way to order your major points?

COHERENCE: TRANSITIONS BETWEEN PARAGRAPHS

Like a paragraph, an essay must also be coherent. Each body paragraph must flow smoothly, and there should also be smooth connections between the (body) paragraphs. One way to achieve this is to use transition words or phrases to guide the reader from one paragraph to another.

Go back to the essay "The Benefits of Living Alone," on page 95, and identify the transition words or phrases that join the paragraphs of the essay.

    The first body paragraph is introduced with the word _____.

    The second body paragraph begins with the expression _____

    The last body paragraph begins with _____.

Depending on the type of writing, transitions for the first body paragraph of an essay may include words and phrases like these:

- First,
- The first advantage of /reason that / example
- One advantage of / reason that / example

    Example sentence: **The first reason that I admire my grandmother so much is that she has worked hard all of her life.**

Transitions for the second body paragraph of an essay may include words and phrases like these:

- Another advantage/reason/example

- An additional advantage/reason
- Second,
- Also,

> *Example sentence:* **Also, my grandmother has always kept her religious faith, which makes me admire her.**

Transitions for the last body paragraph of an essay may include words and phrases like these:

- The last/final advantage /reason /example
- Third,
- Finally,
- Most important,
- The most significant/important/interesting advantage/reason

> *Example sentence:* **Most important, my grandmother has always put her family ahead of herself.**

Exercise 5.6 Using the sample transition words and phrases above, write three possible topic sentences that present three qualities that you admire in a particular person. Check your sentences with a partner.

Writing

Using the ideas you have gathered and the vocabulary, structures, and skills presented in this chapter, write a short essay about your hero or the person you most admire. If you write about a hero from your culture, consider that your audience will probably not be familiar with this person. Identify the person by name and describe his or her accomplishments.

Using the outline on page 96 as a model, first write an outline for your essay. Be sure to include a thesis statement, topic sentences, and supporting details.

In the essay give the major reasons you admire this person. Be sure to include specific details to prove your major points.

Building Language Skills

VOCABULARY: USING NOUNS OR ADJECTIVES
When you write about someone you admire, you will probably write about his or her qualities or characteristics.

You can write about characteristics using either nouns or adjectives:

> *adjective*   *noun*
> **Sam is very *patient*. His *patience* is most obvious when he is talking to his children.**
>
>   *adjective*
> **My brother has always been the most *clever* in our family. One example of his *cleverness* is that he knows how to make money without working very hard.**
>
> **I admire Sam for his *sincerity*. He is *sincere* in all his relationships.**
>
> **My mother's *calmness* is one of her most impressive qualities. She stays *calm* in even the worst situations.**
>
> **My sister is my hero because she is so *energetic*. She transmits this *energy* to everyone who is around her.**

Which of the italicized words are adjectives? Which are nouns?

Exercise 5.7 Use the following adjectives and nouns in sentences of your own. Write them on a separate piece of paper.

friendly	determined	generous
friendliness	determination	generosity
honest	optimistic	
honesty	optimism	

VOCABULARY: USING ACTION VERBS

Writers often rely too heavily on the verb *be*. This is natural since a sentence with *be* is one of the first structures you learn. However, as you become a more experienced writer, you should try to use verbs other than *be*.

The verb *be* is not a strong verb, and other verbs carry a lot more meaning.

Look at these sentences:

> **Mr. Akihiro is a good teacher.**

> Mr. Akihiro **teaches** well.
> He **explains** new material so that it is interesting and easy to understand.
> He **listens** carefully to students.
> He **answers** questions clearly and patiently.
> He **makes** the class fun.

Which sentences do you like best? Why?

The sentences with verbs other than *be* tell what Mr. Akihiro *does* as a good teacher.

Exercise 5.8 Write sentences with verbs other than *be* for the following subjects:

1. My mother is wonderful. (What does she do that makes her wonderful?)

    My mother _____

    _____

    _____

2. My friend Chen is fun to be with. (What does he do that makes him fun to be with?)

    _____

    _____

    _____

3. (Name of a person) is interesting. (What does he/she do that makes him/her interesting?)

    _____

    _____

    _____

SENTENCE PATTERNS: SUBORDINATION

In chapter 2, you learned how to write a sentence with an adverbial clause of time.

> **Whenever** I have a problem, I know that my uncle will help me find the solution.

> He passed the TOEFL **after** he had studied English for two years.

In the first sentence, *whenever* is a subordinator that introduces the dependent (subordinate) clause. In the second sentence, the subordinator is *after*. The subordinate clause cannot stand alone; it must be connected to a main clause.

Also, the dependent clause can come before or after the main clause. However, when the dependent clause comes first, you should put a comma after it.

> **Since I met Mr. Alvaro, I have learned to appreciate many simple things.**

> **I have learned to appreciate many simple things since I met Mr. Alvaro.**

In addition to subordinators to introduce adverbial clauses of time, there are subordinating conjunctions to introduce adverbial clauses of cause and effect, opposition, and condition.

Time	Cause/Effect	Opposition	Condition
after	because	although	if
before	since	even though	whether (or not)
when	as	while	unless
while		whereas	
as			
until			
since			

Notice how some of the other subordinators are used:

I admire Ms. Jones **because** she gives unselfishly of herself.

Although New York City's streets are congested, it is easy to get around on the subways.

Someone is always willing to give you directions **if** you get lost.

In each of these sentences, which is the main clause? Which is the subordinate clause?

VERB TENSE IN SUBORDINATION

For Writing Assignment 2, you may want to write sentences with subordinate clauses to describe someone you admire. Here are two examples:

My friend Frank always **controls** himself when he **gets** angry.

If my mother **needs to make** a decision, she always **thinks** carefully about the consequences.

In these sentences, the simple present tense verb is used in both the main clause and the subordinate clause to describe the habitual action of each person.

When you write sentences with subordinate clauses that express times other than the present, however, you must pay attention to the choice of verb tenses.

Look at these example sentences:

Bilal had been an engineer in Turkey before he came here.

Kyung Hee has made many friends since she moved to the dormitory.

If it begins to rain, we will move the party inside.

While Linh was standing in line to register for classes, she met an old friend from Saigon.

Whenever I forget my umbrella, it rains.

What is the time frame of each sentence? Which verb tense is used in the main clause? in the subordinate clause? Why?

Clearly, writing sentences with subordinate clauses requires you to follow certain rules about verb-tense use. Consult your grammar textbook or your instructor to help you choose which verb tenses to use.

Exercise 5.9   With a partner, read the paragraph below. Find the sentences that contain a main clause plus a subordinate clause. Underline the subordinator, and circle the verb tenses in both clauses. Discuss with your partner these questions. What is the time of each sentence? Why is each verb tense used?

My Determined Friend

My friend Joan is a determined person who has worked hard to achieve her dream of being a journalist. When she was a child, Joan always wanted to write for a newspaper. She dreamed of being a famous journalist even though it seemed like a difficult feat to accomplish. However, she did not give up. She worked on her college newspaper while she was getting a degree in journalism. Since she graduated from college, she has worked for several newspapers, moving up from small-town to big-city papers. Now, she manages a news bureau for the United Press International wire service in New Orleans. If Joan wants to become even more successful in her journalism career, she will. I admire her because she has the determination to reach her goal.

VERB FORMS

Exercise 5.10   Read the paragraph below and edit the underlined verbs. Some of the verbs contain errors in form; others are correct.

My Decision to Leave Home

Five months ago, I had a difficult decision to make. I had to decide whether to stay in Moscow or go to New York and change my life. I chose New York. When I lived in Russia, I have a comfortable life and a good job at the Kodak company in Moscow. I have many friends there. But my most difficult decision was to leave my boyfriend in Moscow. Although I thought about this problem for many days and nights, I couldn't make a clear choice. If I got married in Moscow, I couldn't go to New York with my family. If I stayed with my boyfriend, I can't see my parents anymore. Moscow has a strict law about immigration. Many friends gave me advice, but each person said different things. My mamma told me that I should go with my parents because I need to continue my education and I was too young for married life. My boyfriend told me that I needed to stay with him. At that time, he don't want to move to America since he has a good job and he never left his native land. Fortunately, before I quit my job, I had an important conversation with my boss which helped me reach a decision. I listened to my boss, since he is a strong and capable man. Because he had previously lived in America for 14 years, he advised me about my chances here. "If your boyfriend sincerely love you, you can endure great difficulties and your love will survive," he said. I will remember this conversation my whole life. Finally, I decide to go with my family. I don't know whether my action was right or wrong, but I hope I can be happy and successful in America.

Anna Novikova
Russia

Revising

After writing the first draft of your essay about your hero or the person you admire the most, reread your essay. Then, exchange papers with a partner, and evaluate each other's papers using the Writing Checklist questions below.

Writing Checklist

1. Is the thesis statement clearly written? Does it express the main idea of the whole essay?
2. Does each body paragraph have a topic sentence?
3. Are there enough examples or details to prove the major points?
4. Are there smooth transitions within and between paragraphs?

Journal Writing

Imagine a situation in which you have to be a hero. Describe the situation and tell exactly what you would do. Write two pages about it in your journal.

More Writing Topics

1. Write an essay about the disadvantages or advantages of being a student.
2. Write an essay about the disadvantages or advantages of practicing a certain sport.
3. Write an essay about the qualities of a good partner—a girlfriend or boyfriend, wife or husband.

Chapter 6

Learning New Skills

What special skills have you learned in your life?

What skills are you learning at present?

Sharing a Special Skill

Getting Ideas

BRAINSTORMING

Each of us has special skills that make us different from others. Some of us can tune-up an automobile; others can make friends easily; and still others can prepare a five-course dinner for twenty people. In a small group, talk about the special skills that you have learned from different sources in your life: work, parents, siblings, friends, school, free time, sports, and so on.

Are these skills that others in your group are familiar with? Are these skills that others find unusual or interesting?

Write down the special skills you have.

_____

_____

Next, have one group member report to the class about the special abilities of your group.

Are there skills your classmates have that you would be especially interested in learning? Tell your classmates which skills interest you the most. This will help members of your writing community choose their topics for the next writing assignment.

Writing

FREEWRITING

Think of a simple recipe from your country or from another country that you know well. Imagine that you want to explain to someone in your class how to make this dish.

Spend five minutes writing a list of steps that tell how to make it. If you do not know how to make the dish, write for five minutes about a time you remember when a family member or a friend made it.

The members of your class may not be familiar with some of the special ingredients or utensils used to make the dish. If you do not know the names in English, explain them as well as you can, or give the name in your language and explain it in English.

When you finish, read the writing you have done and make quick revisions in the places where you think the process may be unclear.

Then, continue to write your recipe for another five minutes.

When you have finished, share your writing with a partner. Discuss each other's recipes.

Getting Ideas

BRAINSTORMING

Now, choose one of the special skills you generated on page 112. Focus on a skill that you know very well and that you can explain with authority, in detail, to the class. Choose a skill that few class members share so that you will be showing them how to do something new and interesting.

Write a list of steps involved in the process, following these guidelines:

- Be sure to include all the necessary steps in the order in which they occur.

- Explain the materials required. If there are materials or tools that your audience is not familiar with, explain them. For instance, if you are explaining how to change the oil in a car, you will need to define what an oil filter is.

- Also, when you tell someone how to do something, you sometimes have to warn them what *not* to do. Think of warnings your reader might need. For example, in explaining to a reader how to change the oil in a car, you may want to warn the reader not to put too much oil in the car.

After you write your list of steps, definitions, and warnings, have a partner read your list and have him or her answer these questions:

1. Is the process complete? Are all the steps there, and are they clear? If not, ask your partner to explain the process in more detail. (Remember that you should be able to do the process after you have read the steps.)

2. Are there any terms that you don't understand—for example, the names of ingredients or of tools needed? If so, ask your partner to explain them.

3. Are there places in the process where you think warnings might be needed? Give your partner suggestions.

Composing

ORGANIZING A PROCESS ESSAY

Writing about a process often requires several steps and some detail, so for this writing assignment you will write an essay.

First, look at your freewriting from page 112. From that information, write an outline, using the following outline as a guide.

I.	Introduction	What is the skill? Why is this a skill that the reader would want to learn? Is it fun? Is it easy? What skills does the reader need to do it? (In your thesis statement, tell your readers what skill you will explain. You may also include major steps in the process in the main-idea sentence.)
	Example thesis	**Making a delicious cake is easy if you follow these steps.**
II.	Body paragraph 1	How does the reader begin? What materials does he or she need? What tools or equipment are needed?
	Example topic sentence	**First, gather all the ingredients for the cake.**
	Supporting points	
	Example	**You will need all-purpose flour, sugar, eggs, oil, vanilla extract, and baking powder.**
III.	Body paragraph 2	What is the first part of the process? Where are warnings needed?
	Example topic sentence	**Next, you must mix the ingredients carefully to make the batter.**
	Supporting points	
IV.	Body paragraph 3	What is the next part of the process? Warnings?
	Example topic sentence	**Finally, you are ready to bake the cake.**
	Supporting points	
V.	Conclusion	What are the final steps of the process? What is the end result? Why will the reader enjoy using this skill? What will he or she gain from learning this skill?

After your teacher or classmate has reviewed your outline, read the sample essay below.

The following essay explains how to care for a pet. With your classmates, answer the questions that follow.

Gerbil Care

Most people think rodents like mice and rats would make undesirable pets. But gerbils, hamsters, and guinea pigs are sweet animals. They make good pets because they're fun to watch and simple to take care of. Caring for gerbils is easy if you follow these steps.

First, go to your local pet shop and buy the biggest cage you can find. A good example of a cage is a fish tank. You can buy a plastic gerbil cage, but the gerbils will eventually chew it up, so it's better to get a glass tank. The second thing that you need is gerbil bedding, which is shredded bark. The gerbils chew on the bedding and sleep under it. After two or three days, the bedding multiplies because of how the gerbils chew it up and spread it around. They like to move their bedding until it's the way they want it. You will need to clean their cage and replace the bedding about once a month.

Next, you need to buy seeds, nuts, wheat pellets, and oat grains for the gerbils to eat. You can buy these at a pet shop. You can also buy little gerbil treats. It may seem nice to put the food in a cup or bowl, but since the gerbils will eventually cover it with their bedding, you should just put a small handful of food in a corner of their tank daily. Of course, gerbils need water, too. You should use a water tank because if you put the water in a cup or bowl, the gerbils will also cover it with bedding, and this will make it hard to drink.

Because gerbils have unique chewing habits, you also need to provide things for them to chew on. They have to chew on things, or their teeth will grow too long. They like to chew on cardboard, wood, or plastic. You can buy little wooden bits or cubes at a pet store, or find things around the house that you think the gerbils will like. They especially like toilet-paper rolls or paper-towel rolls. Be careful if you want to take your gerbils out to play because they like to nibble on fingers, too.

In addition, you should buy or make your gerbils a few structures that they can crawl and sleep in. Plastic crawl tubes, penthouses and two-story houses, wooden logs, or cubes with holes in them are sold at pet stores. You may also want to buy a plastic rolling ball big enough for the gerbils to fit in. Put the gerbils in it and let them roll the ball around on a tile or lineoleum floor. You can also make small houses for your gerbils. For instance, take a small cardboard box and cut a hole in it big enough for the gerbils to fit in. The gerbils will kick bedding into the hole, sleep in the box, and then start eating it.

After you read the information I have given you, you will probably want to go to a pet store and buy two gerbils. Don't buy just one; these little critters could die of loneliness. You will have fun watching the gerbils climb up their plastic tubes, eat their small toilet-paper rolls, and sleep in their cardboard boxes. If you take care of your gerbils, they will have a happy home.

Nadia Fellag
U.S.A.

1. What is the main idea of the essay? Where is the thesis statement?

2. Is the process described completely?

3. Underline the topic sentences of each body paragraph. Are the topic sentences well supported with details?

4. What conclusion does the writer draw at the end of the essay?

Writing

Prepare an outline for an essay explaining how to perform a special skill. Keep your audience in mind. Explain clearly what the skill is, how to perform it, and what special tools or ingredients are needed to perform it.

Now you are ready to write your essay, using the outline as well as the knowledge you have gained in this chapter.

Read over the Writing Checklist on page 119 to guide you before you write; then, use it to help you evaluate your writing after you write.

Building Language Skills

PROCESS VERBS: COMMANDS + MODAL AUXILIARY VERBS

Before you begin to share a special skill with your class, consider how you will explain each step of how to perform the process. Read the set of instructions that follow to get some ideas. Answer the question following the instructions with a partner.

Steps for Making a Simple Vanilla Cake

1. Before you start, you must buy the following ingredients: sugar, flour, eggs, vanilla, a lemon, baking powder, and vegetable oil.

2. First, with an electric mixer beat four eggs for two to three minutes until they are fluffy.

3. Then, add one cup of sugar to the eggs. Beat the sugar and eggs together for another two to three minutes.

4. Next, you need to add one teaspoon of vanilla and the grated peel and juice of the lemon and mix them in the batter until it is blended.

5. Mix one cup of all-purpose flour with two teaspoons of baking powder. Add these dry ingredients to the egg-sugar mixture and mix for two minutes.

6. Finally, add one-half cup of vegetable oil to the batter, and mix the batter for two more minutes.

7. You can pour the batter into a large greased and floured pan (9 inches × 12 inches) or into two small pans (9-inch round or square). Bake the cake for thirty minutes in a medium oven (350 degrees Fahrenheit) if you use one pan, or twenty minutes if you use two small pans.

8. Check the cake's doneness by inserting a toothpick into the center of the cake. If the toothpick comes out clean, the cake is done.

9. Let the cake cool ten minutes before removing it from the pan.

Discussion:

1. Is the cake-baking process easy to follow?

2. Can you bake this cake after reading these steps? (If you need additional information, write notes or questions beside the parts that you do not understand.)

3. If you have experience as a cook, can you see places in the instructions where you think inexperienced cooks might have problems? Can you suggest "warnings" to help them complete the process?

4. Underline the verbs used in each sentence. What types of verbs are used? Do all the sentences have subjects? Why or why not?

The recipe you have just read uses two types of verbs: command verbs and modal auxiliary verbs.

Command verbs are commonly used in explaining to someone how to do something.

> *Examples* **Beat four eggs.**
> **Add one cup of sugar to the eggs.**

In this sentence pattern, the subject, *you,* is understood but not stated. The verb is in the simplest form. Use this form to show when a step in a process is necessary.

Modal auxiliary verbs also tell the reader what to do. The simple modal verb pattern is used.

> *Examples* **You need to add one teaspoon of vanilla.**
> **You must bake the cake for thirty minutes.**

In modal-verb sentences, the subject is stated, and the verb is formed by using the modal auxiliary plus the simple form of the verb. In process writing, the two modal auxiliaries illustrated above (*need to* and *must*) indicate necessity. Other modal auxiliaries typically used in process writing include *can* and *may,* which indicate choice of action or possibility of action; and *should* or *ought to,* which indicate recommended action.

Find examples of each type of modal auxiliary in the cake recipe.

Exercise 6.1 Think about how to prepare for a party. With a partner, make a list of steps for the process on a separate piece of paper. Make sure that you include all the steps involved.

Afterwards, look over the steps you wrote. Which sentences contain command verbs? Which contain modal auxiliary verbs? Did you use other types of verbs?

Exercise 6.2 Fill in the blanks to complete the following paragraph. You may use the command form of the verb or subjects and modal auxiliary verbs. After you finish, compare your word choices with those of a partner.

A Parent's Special Skill

Changing a baby's diaper is an easy process if you follow these simple steps. First, _____ a disposable diaper, wet cloths to clean the baby's bottom, and some baby powder. _____ all these materials next to the baby before you start. _____ the baby on a flat surface, such as a bed or a clean floor. _____ the baby's clothing. _____ the baby's old diaper, fold it up, and set it aside. _____ the baby's bottom with the wet cloths. Then, _____ the baby's legs by holding both of its feet up, and _____ the diaper under the baby. The disposable diaper has two large ends: one with stick-on tapes on each side, and the other with no tapes. _____ the end with the tapes under the baby's waist. _____ the baby down onto the diaper. _____ baby powder on the baby's bottom. _____ the other end over the front of the baby. Then, _____ the two ends by opening the stick-on tapes on each side and attaching them to the front end of the diaper. If the baby starts to cry, _____ it. Now, you are finished with the process. All of these steps take only a few minutes, and once you have done it, it will be much easier the second time.

PRONOUN CONSISTENCY

In process writing, you are explaining how to perform a skill, such as playing a game. You have a choice of which person to use, but most commonly you speak directly to a person by using *you* or command-verb forms.

Look at this sentence from "Gerbil Care":

You can buy a plastic gerbil cage, but the gerbils will eventually chew it up.

It is possible to express this idea in other ways:

A person can buy a plastic gerbil cage, but the gerbils will eventually chew it up.

One can buy a plastic gerbil cage, but the gerbils will eventually chew it up.

Which of the three sentences appeals to you?

You is considered less formal than *one* and *a person*, so you might want to choose the latter two expressions in very formal writing situations. However, all of them are acceptable; the most important thing is to be consistent in your choice of pronouns. When using pronouns, it is essential to remember that a pronoun must agree in number and gender (sex) with its referent (the word or phrase to which it refers).

Look at these sentences:

they   their

When women want to lose weight, she should change her diet.

it

Although I read all the information in the books, I couldn't use them.

One common mistake that writers make is not being consistent when they are using personal pronouns. It is important to be consistent and not to jump from one person to another. For example, if you are talking about men, you should use *they* and *them* and *their* to refer to the men. If you are talking about a man, you should use *he* and *him* and *his*. If you switch pronouns without a reason, the reader will not be able to follow your writing easily.

Exercise 6.3 Read the following paragraph and correct any inconsistencies in pronoun use.

A person makes many important decisions in his life. First, they must decide what field of study to major in. When making this decision, he should think about what kind of job they would like to have in the future. They should consider whether they enjoy working with people, with machines, or with numbers. Second, you must choose whether to get married or not. You have to decide whether you want a partner to share your life with or whether you prefer to live on her own. Finally, he decides about having children. If they opt to have children, they must think about when and how many. Life is a constant series of decisions, but these are the most important ones that a person makes.

Revising

With a partner, share your essay explaining how to perform a special skill, and evaluate each other's papers by answering the questions on the Writing Checklist below.

Writing Checklist

1. Does the introductory paragraph invite the reader to learn the special skill that your partner is explaining?
2. Is the process complete? Are there any trouble spots that need clarifying?
3. Are process verbs used and formed correctly?
4. Is the use of pronouns consistent?

A Game from Your Culture

Getting Ideas

BRAINSTORMING

With your class, brainstorm games you play now or played as children. Think of games from your country and games played worldwide. Select one game that is unfamiliar to many of your classmates. Your choice of game could be a sport, another type of outdoor game, or an indoor game; it could be a game played with a group or alone.

Choose a partner from a culture outside of yours. Tell the partner how to play your game. Then, make a list of "steps" involved in playing your game. Share the list with your partner.

Answer these questions as you read your partner's list of steps:

1. Can you play the game after reading the steps? If not, decide what steps are unclear or which parts of the game are incomplete or unclear. In the margin of your partner's list write notes about what you do not understand or about which points are incomplete.

2. Are there places in the process where you think warnings might be needed? Write suggestions for your partner on his or her paper.

3. Are there any terms (for example, pieces of equipment, tools, and so on) that you or your partner don't know how to express in English? If so, consult your instructor.

Discuss each other's papers. Make changes and add information where it is necessary.

READING

Read the following essay, paying attention to its organization.

Playing S Hop

A popular fighting game in Japan is *S* Hop. In this game, players try to conquer their opponents' headquarters. It's an easy, exciting game, played by following these steps.

To begin, you need at least four people, two empty cans, and a wide place. To prepare an *S* Hop court, make a large *S* on the ground with chalk. The two circles of the *S* are each group's headquarters. Set a can in the top part of each circle. Make a safety zone near the entry of each *S* circle. This zone can be used by any member of your team, but just one team member should stay there at a time. Next, divide the players into two groups. One member of each team should guard his team's safety zone. The other team members should stand near the safety zone. Now, you are ready to play.

First, you must know how to attack your opponents' headquarters. The winner of the game is the person who kicks the opponents' can out of their headquarters, so this involves attacking the enemy. When you leave your territory, you must hop on one foot while standing outside. If you meet an enemy outside, you can attack him by pushing his body with your hand. However, if your other foot touches the ground during the attack, you die. After you have attacked and "killed" an opponent by pushing or dragging him out of your safety zone, you can retreat to your team's position near the safety zone. At this time, you can stand on both legs and no one can attack you. Then, you can advance back into the enemy's territory on both legs and kick the can out of their headquarters. However, if you are pushed out of the opponent's circle by an enemy player, you die.

Second, you must know how to defend your headquarters. If all of your team's players are kicked out of your circle by your opponents, your platoon is defeated. Therefore, a member of your team should always remain within the circle to defend the headquarters. A "garrison" of your teammates can attack an invading enemy player by pushing him out or dragging him over the circle line. This enemy is then "dead."

In conclusion, the game requires strategy because if no one on your team stays within your team's circle, your headquarters is destroyed. Your enemy then has two safety zones and the contest is over. Of course, this is a fighting game, so you may get hurt. But it's a very exciting game. Furthermore, it doesn't require any special equipment. You can enjoy this game at any place and at any time.

Ryo Sano
Japan

Composing

OUTLINING

Using the list you prepared in brainstorming, make an outline for your essay about a game. Use the sample outline on page 114 as well as the sample essays "Gerbil Care" and "Playing *S* Hop" as guides.

INTRODUCTORY PARAGRAPH

Look over the essay "Playing *S* Hop."

This essay follows basically the same outline that you used to write about your special skill in chapter 5. However, notice that in the introductory paragraph, the writer also explains the object, or goal, of the game. It's a good idea to include this information in the introduction of this type of process essay so that the reader can understand the purpose of all the steps.

The introductory paragraph must introduce the topic of the essay and present the thesis statement (the main idea) of the essay. Because the introduction is the first part of the essay that the reader sees, it should also catch the reader's interest so that he or she will want to keep reading.

There are several devices that you can use to make your introduction inviting to the reader. You might do the following:

1. Emphasize the importance of a topic

2. Ask a question

3. Tell an anecdote, or story

4. Use a quotation

5. Describe a shared experience

6. Use the "funnel" approach illustrated below; that is, begin with general ideas about the topic and narrow the ideas into the specific point of the thesis statement

7. Use a "turnabout"; that is, begin with a view that is the opposite of the one you present in the thesis statement

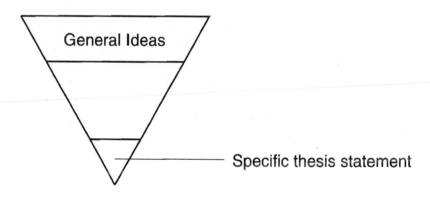

"Funnel" Approach

Whatever device you choose, be careful not to start too generally. Don't begin with ideas that are too far away from the idea of your thesis statement. If, for example, you are writing about how to play a game, do not begin by saying, "In the world there are many forms of entertainment."

One way to make sure you don't begin the introduction in the wrong place is to use one key word or phrase (or a synonymous phrase) from your thesis statement in the first or second sentence of the introduction. For example, an introduction with a thesis statement about how to play a specific game should contain the word *game* or the idea of "game" in the first or second sentence.

Remember also that the thesis statement is generally placed at or near the end of the introductory paragraph.

Exercise 6.4   Reread the introduction of "Gerbil Care," on page 115, and orally answer these questions:

What is the topic?

What is the thesis statement?

What device(s) are used to catch the reader's interest?

Which word or phrase is found in both the first or second sentence and in the thesis statement?

Exercise 6.5   Look at the introductions in the following exercise, and answer the questions that follow each of them.

1.   Homesickness is a real disease, and it affects most people who move to a new country. If you suffer from homesickness, you miss your family, your friends, certain foods, in fact, everything about your country. Nothing in your new environment gives you any pleasure or excitement. All you see is darkness, and all you feel is a sadness and loneliness about being so far from home. Fortunately, homesickness doesn't have to be a permanent illness. If you follow these easy steps, you can overcome homesickness and be on your way to a happier and more successful life in your new surroundings.

What is the topic?

What is the thesis statement?

What device(s) are used to catch the reader's interest?

Which word or phrase is found in both the first or second sentence and in the thesis statement?

2.   What's the most important thing in your life? If you think about it for a few minutes, you are likely to answer, "my health." Most people would agree that physical and mental well-being are vital to a happy and productive life. If it is so important, then we must be sure to take care of it. What is the key to maintaining good health? It's as simple as remembering to eat well, to get plenty of rest, to exercise, and to avoid certain activities.

What is the topic?

What is the thesis statement?

What device(s) are used to catch the reader's interest?

Which word or phrase is found in both the first or second sentence and in the thesis statement?

Exercise 6.6   Write an introduction for your essay. Review the examples above. When you have finished, exchange introductions with a partner and discuss the questions from Exercise 6.5. Revise your introduction as necessary.

Writing

Use your outline and introductory paragraph as well as other knowledge you have learned in this chapter to write an essay about a game from your culture. Consider your audience as you write. The game you are describing may be unfamiliar to members of your class, so explain it clearly and carefully. Refer to the Writing Checklist on page 119 before and after you write.

Building Language Skills

VOCABULARY OF GAMES

You can use certain universal terms to describe the action, players, and materials you use in a game.

rules	strategy	team	goal	win/winner
points	score	steps	lose/loser	play/player
equipment				

Think about your own game, the place it's played, the players, the actions, and the materials. The terms you use vary, depending on the game you are explaining. For instance, in tennis, the place you play is called a *court*, and in baseball, it's called a *field*.

Exercise 6.7 Before you write an essay about a game from your culture, generate the particular vocabulary words you will need in order to explain your game. Consult your instructor if you need assistance.

Place:_____

Players: _____

Opponents: _____

Materials: _____

GERUNDS AND INFINITIVES

Gerunds (verb + -*ing*) and infinitives (*to* + verb) are verb forms used as nouns. Like nouns, they can be used as subjects and objects in a sentence. Gerunds and infinitives are useful to explain a process in writing. The actions that you describe in playing a game or doing a skilled activity can be subjects or objects in a sentence.

Look at these sentences from "Gerbil Care":

> *Example*   **Caring** for gerbils is easy if you follow these steps.
> [Gerbils] like **to chew** on cardboard, wood, or plastic.

What is the subject of the first sentence? What is the main verb? In the second sentence, what is the main verb? What is the object?

In the first sentence, the gerund *caring* is the subject of the main verb *is*. In the second sentence, the infinitive *to chew* is the object of the main verb *like*.

You probably already use gerunds and infinitives commonly in your writing. However, you may have problems as you try to decide which of the forms to use. Here are some guidelines to help you:

1. Gerunds, not infinitives, are commonly used as subjects of sentences. Gerund subjects take singular verbs.

   > *Example*   **Playing** mahjong **is** a popular pastime in Hong Kong.

2. Gerunds are used as objects of certain verbs in sentences.

   > *Example*   As a child, I enjoyed **flying** kites.

3. Gerunds are used as objects of prepositions.

   > *Example*   One purpose **of learning** to cook well is to save money.
   > (The object of the preposition *of* is the gerund *learning*.)

4. Infinitives can be used as subjects, but it's more common to begin with a dummy *it* subject followed by the infinitive.

   > *Example*   **To drive** a car is easy.   (unusual order)
   > It's easy **to drive** a car.   (more common)

5. Infinitives are used as objects of certain verbs in sentences.

    Example   You can learn **to speak** English more easily if you make English-speaking friends.

6. Infinitives without *to* are used as objects of certain verbs such as *let, make,* and *have.*

    Example   **Let** the cake cool for thirty minutes.
(The verb *let* is followed by the bare infinitive verb form, *cool,* as the object of the sentence.)

For a complete list of verbs that are followed by gerunds, infinitives, or bare infinitives, consult your grammar textbook.

Exercise 6.8   Read the introduction paragraph below. With a partner, underline the gerunds and infinitives. Then, make a list of five sentences that suggest how a person could accomplish the skill described. Use gerunds or infinitives in your sentences if appropriate.

    For some people, one of the most difficult skills is the art of making "small talk" at parties. Making "small talk" means talking easily about unimportant subjects, often to people that you do not know. At a party, you often meet new people, and after you are introduced, you want to find something to say. You may talk about the weather, politics, the party itself, the city or its surroundings—any "small" topic that does not "invade" the stranger's privacy. You can learn to develop the art of "small talk" by following these easy steps.

    Example   **You can begin by introducing yourself.**

1. _____

2. _____

3. _____

4. _____

5. _____

SENTENCE FOCUS

In chapter 3, you learned that your sentences should begin with a clear, logical focus. You learned that you should think about what or who you are writing about and try to make that the subject of your sentence.

Look at these two sentences.

    Confidence helped me know that I could pull down the weight machine.

    I had confidence that I could pull down the weight machine.

Which sentence is clearer? Why?

The second sentence is clearer because the subject is personal rather than abstract. In the second sentence, the writer focuses on a personal subject (*I*) and what he did (*had confidence.*)

Exercise 6.9 Read the following sentences, which are awkward and sometimes illogical because they do not start with the most appropriate subjects. Using the logical subject, rewrite the sentences to make them clearer.

Unfocused: **In college exists the American way of choosing subjects, which I prefer.**

Focused: **I prefer the American way of choosing subjects in college.**

1. Unfocused: Music has a function which releases our emotions.

   Focused:_____

2. Unfocused: Sometimes problems are possible for us to ask our families for help, but some are not.

   Focused:_____

3. Unfocused: Receiving gifts has always been appreciated by myself.

   Focused:_____

4. Unfocused: The time is more than 1500 years ago when their work was inscribed on stone.

   Focused:_____

5. Unfocused: The idea of a smart person has many characteristics.

   Focused:_____

6. Unfocused: Due to my hard work and dedication earned me the best manager of the year award.

   Focused:_____

7. Unfocused: First of all, to be a businesswoman can earn a lot of money.

   Focused:_____

Revising

After you have written the first draft of your essay explaining how to play a game from your culture, have a partner read and revise it.

Have your partner consider the questions from the Writing Checklist on the next page.

Revise your essay as needed.

Journal Writing

A. Write one page about one of these topics.

1. Write about your experience in learning a skill from a person. Focus more on how you learned, rather than on what you learned.

2. Explain a skill that you would like to learn. Tell why you would like to learn it.

B. Then, write one page on any topic or topics of your choice.

More Writing Topics

1. Write an essay to explain how to plan a vacation to a particular destination.

2. Write an essay to explain how to make friends in a new city.

3. Write an essay to explain how to perform a skill or complete a process from your field of study.

Chapter 7

Changes

What personal changes do you need to make in your life?

What changes are needed in your community? your hometown?

Is change always positive?

A Personal Change

Getting Ideas

READING/SONG
Read the lyrics of the song and answer the questions that follow.

Man in the Mirror*

I'm gonna make a change,
for once in my life.
It's gonna feel real good,
gonna make a difference,
gonna make it right.

As I turned up the collar
on my favorite winter coat,
this wind is blowing my mind.
I see the kids in the street
with not enough to eat.
Who am I to be blind,
pretending not to see their need.
I saw this disregard,
a broken bottle top
and a one-man show.
They follow each other on the wind, you know,
'cause they got nowhere to go.

That's why I want you to know:

Chorus:
I'm starting with the man in the mirror.
I'm asking him to change his ways.
And no message could've been any clearer.
If you wanna make the world
a better place, take a look at
yourself. Then make a change.

I've been a victim of
a selfish kind of love.
It's time that I realize
that there's love in your home,
not a nickel to loan.
Could it be, could it be,
pretending that they're not alone?

A widow deeply scarred,
somebody's broken heart,
and a washed-out dream.
They follow the pattern of the wind,
you see,
'cause they got no place to be.

That's why I'm starting with me.

Chorus:
You gotta get it while you
got the time.
When you close your heart,
then you close your mind.

Chorus
It's gonna feel real good.
Just let yourself.
You've got to stop it yourself.

Discussion

1. Who is the "man in the mirror"? Who is the "you" in the song?

2. What change are the writers of the song asking you to make?

3. Define the reductions used in the song:

   gonna   'cause   wanna   gotta

4. One line of the chorus says

   **"If you wanna make the world
   a better place, take a look at
   yourself. Then make a change."**

Discuss one specific change you want to make in yourself. How can you do it?

AUDIO/VIDEO

Try to listen to "Man in the Mirror," the title song of Michael Jackson's *Man in the Mirror* audiotape. If the video version of this song is available in your area, view it and make notes of the problems that are visually portrayed. After you listen to the song or view the video, brainstorm with your class a list of major world problems. Write your list here.

_____

_____

_____

BRAINSTORMING

People seek change in their cities and countries as well as in themselves. To explore personal changes you want to make in your life, fill out the chart below. Check all areas in which you want to make a personal change. For example, you might check personality, and write: "I am too shy." For each area you check, write one brief explanation of a change you want to make. Then, share some of your responses in your group.

AREAS OF MY LIFE THAT I WANT TO CHANGE	
Area (✓ for Yes)	Explanation
Personality	
Education	
Family	
Health	
Friends	
Habits	
Love relationships	
Financial status	
Career	

Composing

OUTLINING

In this essay you will describe a personal change that you would like to make. Limit yourself to one aspect, or characteristic of yourself, that you would like to change.

Here are two rough sample outlines for Writing Assignment 1.

Sample Outline 1

I. Introduction: Introduce the topic and state what aspect of yourself you want to change.
Example thesis statement **I would like to stop smoking.**

II. Body paragraph 1: Describe the existing aspect that you want to change.
Example topic sentence **I have been a heavy smoker for five years.**
Supporting points

III.   Body paragraph 2: Describe the steps you can make to change it.
Supporting points

IV.   Body paragraph 3: Describe the potential benefits of this change.
Supporting points

V.   Conclusion: Restate the thesis and make a prediction.

Sample Outline 2

I.   Introduction: Describe the existing aspect of yourself that you want to change.
Example thesis statement   **I want to become more athletic.**

II.   Body Paragraph 1: Give a reason why you want to change it.
Supporting points

III.   Body paragraph 2: Give a second reason why you want to change it.
Supporting points

IV.   Body paragraph 3: Explain how you are going to make the change.
Supporting points

V.   Conclusion: Mention the potential benefits of the change.

When you write your own outline, you should write complete sentences for the thesis statement and topic sentences; include the details you will use to support your major points in phrases or sentences.

READING/OUTLINING

Read the following essay. Then, with your group, answer the questions that follow.

The Effects of Being Overweight

Each person would like to change something in his behavior, character, or physical appearance. Some people hope to have more self confidence; others simply want to feel more comfortable. In my case, I would like to lose weight.

The first reason I want to lose weight is that finding appropriate clothing is a nightmare when I am overweight. I can't follow the fashion because it is designed for slim people. Sometimes, I go shopping for a dress and I don't get one I want because the shape isn't suitable to my thick waist. As a result, I feel disappointed and I am angry about my weight. Once, I tried on a pair of beautiful white pants, but my large thighs made this nice outfit awful on me. Thus, I gave up buying it and, once again, I was furious about my terrible size. Another thing is that I am afraid of trying on beachwear. In short, I hate selecting clothes when I am overweight.

In addition, my weight influences my health. I can't easily practice a sport. For example, I can't do gymnastics exercises because I execute the movements too slowly. I can't keep up with the runners in Memorial Park because I don't have enough breath. In the same way, for me climbing stairs is as difficult as riding a bicycle up a hill. Furthermore, doctors declare that most fat people will have heart problems because fat causes a thickening of blood. In other words, my excess weight is not compatible with good health.

It is clear that I must take steps to lose weight. I have different solutions to accomplish this goal. First, I'm going to go on a diet by following the instructions of a book which is titled *How to Lose Weight and Eat Normally*. The diet forbids the mixture of glucosides and lipids. Also, this book advises eating a lot of fiber. Second, I'm used to eating too much when I'm nervous or anxious, so I must learn to relax, to accept quietly the problems of everyday life. For instance, I must avoid losing my temper when my daughter comes back home too late or doesn't clean her bedroom. The third thing absolutely necessary to succeed on a diet is to exercise daily or three times a week. In sum, I must be able to lose weight by going on a diet, relaxing, and doing sports.

In conclusion, I have good reasons for losing weight. Although it might not be easy at first, controlling my weight will bring me a lot of benefits such as good health and good looks. In my opinion, losing weight is for me one of the best ways to improve myself.

Chantal Gorin
France

Discussion

1. What is the thesis statement?

2. Which of the two suggested outlines does this essay follow?

Exercise 7.1   With your class, outline the first two body paragraphs of this essay. Then, with a partner, continue the outline. Include the details that the writer uses to support her topic sentences.

THESIS STATEMENT: ESSAY ABOUT CHANGE

Look at these two models of an introductory paragraph. Find the thesis statement in each.

When I was a child, I watched my mother cook from the dining room, but I rarely entered the kitchen. The few times that I asked to help her prepare meals were disasters. I often cut my fingers, spilled ingredients on the floor, or made my mother very nervous. Consequently, I never learned how to cook. However, now that I'm living on my own, I find that I have no choice; I am determined to become a good cook.

Air pollution is a problem throughout the world, but in Los Angeles it is almost intolerable. As you drive into the city, you are struck by the brown cloud of pollution hanging overhead. When you walk in the city, your eyes begin to water and itch. After a few hours, you find yourself breathing with difficulty and coughing. How can people continue to live here? The city must take action to control the air-pollution nightmare.

In each introduction, the last sentence of the paragraph presents the thesis, or main idea. Both thesis statements present the change the writer wants to make.

In Chapter 6, you learned about different devices that are used in the introductory paragraph. Review this lesson on pages 121-122.

Which device or devices are used in each of the introductions above?

Each of these introductions starts with general ideas about the topic that lead into what the writer wants to say about it—the thesis statement. In the first introduction, the general topic is cooking. The writer begins the introduction by telling a story about her cooking; this leads into the thesis statement, which contains the controlling idea—that the writer wants to learn to be a good cook.

In the second introduction, the general topic is air pollution in Los Angeles. The writer begins by emphasizing the importance of the topic and ends with the thesis statement, which expresses the controlling idea—that the government should improve the pollution situation.

Exercise 7.2   Choose four areas of your life that you want to change from the Brainstorming activity on page 132. Write a thesis statement for each area of change. Be sure that your thesis statement presents the topic and the controlling idea (what you want to say about the topic).

> *Example explanation*   **I am too shy.**
>
> *Example thesis statement*   **To be happier and more successful, I must become less shy.**

Exercise 7.3   For one of the thesis statements you wrote above, write an introduction paragraph. Begin with a sentence that presents the general topic, and follow with sentences that logically lead into what you want to say about the topic—the thesis statement.

RETURN SENTENCE

Good writers often end a body paragraph with a sentence that restates the main idea of the topic sentence. This sentence is called a return sentence.

With this final sentence, the writer can remind the reader of the main point of his or her paragraph. This is a better way of closing your paragraph than simply ending with the last piece of specific support.

Look back at the first body paragraph of "The Effects of Being Overweight" on page 133. Find the topic sentence and the support. Does the writer include a return sentence as well? What is it?

Reread the second and third body paragraphs of the same essay. Find the topic sentences and the return sentences.

OUTLINING: PEER REVIEW

Below is an outline for a student's paper about a personal change.

I.   Introduction:
Thesis: I need to improve my study habits.

II.   Topic sentence: I have some bad study habits.

    A.   lack enough concentration in class

    B.   lack real understanding of what teacher says

C.   lie down when I read

D.   watch TV and read

III.   Topic sentence: It should be easy for me to change these poor habits if I take certain steps.

A.   get more concentration

B.   build logical comprehension

C.   improve my study atmosphere

IV.   Topic sentence: If I change my study habits, I will see some benefits.

A.   get better grades

B.   improve my learning efficiency

C.   protect my vision

Although the main ideas in this outline are clear and well organized, a good reviewer will have questions for the writer. These questions should help the writer develop his or her ideas fully and clearly. Here is the same outline with a reviewer's questions added in italics.

I.   Introduction
Thesis statement: I need to improve my study habits.

II.   Topic sentence: I have some bad study habits.

A.   lack enough concentration in class
What do you think about in class?

B.   lack real understanding of what teacher says
Can you give an example of something you have not understood?

C.   lie down when I read
What are you reading? Why is this bad? Do you fall asleep?

D.   watch TV and read
Why is this bad? Can you concentrate? Do you remember what you read?

III.   Topic sentence: It should be easy for me to change these poor habits if I take certain steps.

A.   concentrate more
How will you do this?

B.   check my comprehension
How will you do this? Can you give an example?

C.   Improve my study atmosphere
What will change?

IV.   Topic sentence: If I change my study habits, I will see some benefits.

A.   get better grades
What are your grades now? What do you want them to be?

B.   improve my learning efficiency
Can you explain this or give an example?

C.   protect my vision
How will you protect your vision?

Exercise 7.4   Read the outline that follows. Work with a partner and think of questions about the supporting points you might expect to be answered. Write your questions below each supporting point.

I.   Introduction:
    Thesis: In order to reach my goal of becoming a successful jazz musician in the United States, I need to be more self-disciplined.

II. Topic sentence: I lack discipline in three important areas of my life.
    A. my studies

    _____

    _____

    B. my physical activity

    _____

    _____

    C. my music

    _____

    _____

III. Topic sentence: I must take steps to become more self-disciplined.
    A. make and follow a schedule for my studies

    _____

    _____

    B. exercise more

    _____

    _____

    C. practice my music more

    _____

    _____

IV. Topic sentence: With more self-discipline, I will be able to reach my goal.
   A. learn more English

   _____

   _____

   B. have more strength

   _____

   _____

   C. become a better musician

   _____

   _____

Writing

OUTLINING

Choose a topic for your essay on personal change, and outline the essay following one of the sample outlines on pages 135-136.

Once you have written your outline, exchange it with a partner. Consider the following as you review your partner's outline.

1. Does the thesis statement present the change the writer wants to make?

2. Do the topic sentences clearly announce the focus of each body paragraph?

3. Do the supporting details explain the topic sentences?

4. Is the outline logical?

To help your partner develop his ideas fully, think of the questions you expect to be answered in his essay. Write them on the outline.

Then, write a short essay on personal change.

REVISING

PROOFREADING

Here are some strategies for proofreading:

1. Choose one or two major problems that you have in writing. Proofread only for these major errors.

2. Make sure every sentence has a subject and a verb. Remember that subordinating words (for example, *because, if, when, who, which, that*) introduce dependent clauses that cannot stand by themselves.

Building Language Skills

SENTENCE PATTERNS: SUBORDINATION

Exercise 7.5   Complete the following sentences by adding a main clause or an adverbial clause.

> *Example*   _____, I will be happy.
>
> **If I find a suitable roommate, I will be happy.**
>
> **Although I have no experience with computers, _____.**
>
> **Although I have no experience with computers, I must learn this important skill.**

1. I need to start an exercise program _____.

2. _____
   because I hope to get a good job.

3. _____
   since I want to travel more.

4. _____
   I will try to be more organized.

5. Although I hate to cook and clean, _____.

6. If I stop smoking, _____.

7. I can overcome my shyness _____.

8. If I eat less, _____.

9. I will get higher grades _____.

VOCABULARY: CHOOSING SYNONYMOUS PHRASES

Using synonymous phrases—different words or phrases with the same meaning—makes your writing more varied and interesting. For example, if you want to write about going on a diet, you should not use the words *go on a diet* repeatedly in your essay. Instead, seek out different ways to express the same idea.

Look at these synonymous phrases:

going on a diet	**dieting**
watching my weight	**changing my eating habits**
eating more sensibly	**controlling my eating**

To add more synonymous phrases to your writing, use a thesaurus to find a synonym. Then, check the meaning of the synonym in a dictionary to make sure that is the word you want.

Exercise 7.6   Write a synonymous phrase for the phrases in bold type in each sentence.

   Examples   Becoming a **more serious** student is one change I need to make in myself.

   Becoming a **diligent** student is one change I need to make in myself.

   Its important for me **to be more confident.**
   It's important for me **to gain self-confidence.**

1. My biggest problem is that I'm **very lazy**.

   _____

2. One important change that I should make in my behavior is **to become less dependent on my parents.**

   _____

3. If I plan to continue to study in the United States, I must learn **to spend my money wisely.**

   _____

4. In the future, I want to try **to be less shy.**

   _____

5. Since I would like to work in an import-export company in Taiwan, **I must improve** my English.

   _____

Exercise 7.7   Edit the following paragraph by rewording the words and phrases in bold type, which are overused. You may have to rewrite sentences to add synonymous phrases.

   It is difficult to change a shortcoming. At the beginning, I must make up my mind not to behave the way I usually do, not to be lazy. I will keep on warning myself **not to be lazy** anymore. I will try to imagine how good I will feel when I change this **shortcoming**. Second, I will reward myself for every small change. For example, I will buy myself a CD or a new item of clothing when I **am not lazy.** Third,

I will do my housework that I can do and keep trying to do some morning exercise such as push-ups, jogging, and sit-ups. I must also finish my homework every day. Finally, I will be realistic in the goals I set for myself. I will set small **goals** at first because they are easier to reach.

Wang Cheung Lee
Hong Kong

Revising

After you have written the first draft, or version, of your short essay, have a partner read and revise it. Have your partner consider these Writing Checklist questions.

Writing Checklist

1. Does the essay have an introduction paragraph? Does it have a thesis statement?
2. Does the essay's body follow one of the two outlines suggested on pages 135–136? Does each body paragraph have a topic sentence and relevant support?
3. Does the essay contain a conclusion paragraph?
4. In general, is the organization of the essay logical?
5. Does the writer use synonymous phrases rather than repeating the same words?

A Change in Your Community

Getting Ideas

BRAINSTORMING

With a small group, discuss these questions:

1. What is one aspect of your community, city, or country that you want to change?

2. How did this problem begin? How can this problem be solved?

3. How will your community, city, or country be different after the change is made?

FREEWRITING

1. Think of one specific aspect of your community, city, or country that you wish to change.

2. Write for five minutes about the problem. Focus on describing the problem. As you write, do not stop to correct grammar or spelling, and do not erase. Do not use a dictionary. Write what comes into your mind. Afterwards, stop and read what you have written.

3. Write for five more minutes. Now, write about how the problematic aspect of your community, city, or country can be changed. Focus on the steps that should be taken to make the change.

4. When you have finished, share your writing with a partner from your discussion group. Give each other comments about what you have written.

5. Save this writing for your next assignment.

Composing

CONCLUSIONS

The conclusion is an important part of an essay. It is your last chance to make your point clear. Here are some basic principles you should follow to write an effective conclusion:

1. The conclusion should follow logically from the body of the essay.

2. The conclusion must summarize the whole essay, not just one or two major points.

3. The conclusion should not raise any new points but must be related to the thesis statement or body of the essay.

As with the introductory paragraph, the concluding paragraph will vary depending on the type of essay you write. For an essay suggesting a change, the most logical device to use in the conclusion would be a result, a prediction, or a recommendation. You may want to present the result(s) of your change. Or you may want to predict what will happen if the change occurs.

Look over the essay "The Effects of Being Overweight," on pages 133-134. Which device(s) does the writer use in her conclusion?

Exercise 7.8   Look over the conclusion paragraph that you wrote for the Writing Assignment 1 essay. If necessary, revise it so that it follows the basic principles listed above and presents either a result or a prediction. Share your revised conclusion with a partner and evaluate it.

READING

Read the following essay and decide which of the outlines (pages 135-136) for an essay about change it follows. Also, determine which type of information the writer includes in the conclusion paragraph. Then, outline the essay.

Solving the Traffic Problems in Taipei

If you ask foreigners, "What is the most impressive thing to you in Taipei?" most of them will reply, "Heavy and messy traffic!" In addition, according to a public-opinion poll, the worst problem for inhabitants of Taipei is the congested traffic. These messages show that we can't wait anymore to change the bad traffic situation in Taipei.

The two main reasons for traffic problems in Taipei are the excessive number of vehicles in Taipei and the fact that drivers disobey traffic rules. According to the department of transportation, there are nearly one million cars and motorcycles in Taipei, but the roads of Taipei can't accommodate the large number of vehicles. This condition causes traffic congestion. During rush hour, the average speed of cars is only 15 miles per hour. It may take one hour from my home to school, although the distance is only 10 miles. The excessive number of vehicles also causes parking problems. In Taipei, it is very difficult to find a parking space. Because the drivers disobey the traffic rules, these traffic problems are even worse. They park their cars in the no-parking areas. They change lanes without noticing the cars behind them. They rush ahead without yielding. Consequently, driving a car in Taipei is dangerous and difficult. These factors cause the heavy and messy traffic in Taipei.

There are some methods to solve the traffic problems in Taipei. The government should increase the tax on cars and the price of gas. This policy will increase the expense of having a car. People may decide not to buy a car because of the additional expenses. In this way, we can limit the growth of the number of cars. Furthermore, the government should encourage the inhabitants of Taipei to take mass transportation or carpool to their work places or schools. These methods would decrease the number of cars on the streets of Taipei. The government should also increase the fines for violating traffic rules. High fines can deter drivers from breaking traffic rules. Reeducating the drivers that violate the traffic regulations is also important for reducing the violations.

By solving the traffic problems in Taipei, the citizens will get some benefits. First, they won't need to spend so much time in traffic congestion. They will have more time for work or pleasure, which is important for people in modern society. Second, driving a car in Taipei will be easy, safe, and comfortable. Drivers will yield to others as they obey traffic rules. The good behavior may encourage everyone in Taipei to create a polite and orderly city. Furthermore, foreigners will have a better first impression when they come to Taipei. These changes will be helpful to upgrade the international position of Taipei.

Indeed, Taipei has serious traffic problems. To solve these traffic problems, we not only depend on the determination of the government but also need the cooperation of the inhabitants of Taipei. It will be difficult, but we must try our best to change the traffic situation in Taipei.

I-Chung Chane
Taiwan

OUTLINING

Use one of the two outlines on pages 135–136 to help you plan an essay about a change that you want to make in your community.

As you did for Writing Assignment 1, write an outline that contains the following information:

I.   Introduction
     Thesis statement (Write a complete sentence.)

II.-IV. Body paragraphs
     Topic sentence for each paragraph (Write complete sentences.)
     Support: (Write words or phrases to indicate supporting ideas in each paragraph.)

V.   Conclusion (Write a complete sentence that restates the thesis statement.)

Have your teacher check your outline before your begin writing your essay.

Writing

Use the outline above to guide you as you write an essay about a change that you want to see in one aspect of your community, city, or country. Keep your audience in mind. Many of your classmates may not be familiar with the area you are writing about. Name the place, and include information about its size and location. Be sure to give your paper a title.

Review the Writing Checklist that follows before and after you write.

Building Language Skills

PERSON IN WRITING

In the essay "Solving the Traffic Problems in Taipei," the writer discusses a situation that affects many people, not just himself. Thus, he talks about "drivers," "the government," and "citizens"; and he uses third-person pronouns, *they, them, it,* and *their,* to refer to them. This use of third-person pronouns creates a greater distance between the writer and the subject. For academic writing on nonpersonal topics, it is more appropriate to use third-person pronouns than first- and second-person pronouns.

PRESENT PERFECT TENSE

Read the following paragraph.

The Changes in Me in Recent Years

I have changed a lot in recent years. I used to be a foolish, dependent girl, but now I am a mature and independent woman. I am the youngest child in my family, so when I was growing up, my family did everything for me. I never had to cook or clean or help take care of my brothers and sisters. My parents gave me everything I wanted, so I thought I was the best girl. I thought I was always right, and my family and friends had to listen to me. However, my situation is not the same anymore. Now I am living alone and I am working. Since I began to work, I have changed in several ways. I have learned many things from working. I know there are many people better than me. I realize I was a foolish and snobbish girl. Now, I know how to deal with other people, how to consider other people's positions, and how to act more independently. I am not always perfect, but I am trying. I think these changes are good. As time passes, I know there are many more things I have to learn.

Shu-Huei Liang
Taiwan

Look at the topic sentence of this paragraph: "I have changed a lot in recent years." Notice that the present perfect tense (*have* or *has* + past participle) is used. This tense is very useful when you are writing about things that have happened in the past, but not at a definite time.

Notice the time difference between the sentence above and this sentence:

I changed a lot last year.

The simple past tense is used here to express a past event at a definite time, "last year," as opposed to an indefinite time, "in recent years."

The present perfect tense is also used to describe an action that continues over time from the past to the present, as in this sentence: "Since I began to work, I have changed in several ways." The verb form *have changed* indicates that she started to change when she began to work and that she made changes from that time until the present time.

Look at this sentence from the paragraph:

I have learned many things from working.

Explain why the present perfect tense is used there.

Exercise 7.9   A. Write three sentences about how you have changed since you came to this city or town.

> *Example*   ***I have met many people since I came here.***

1. _____

2. _____

3. _____

B. Write three sentences about how some aspect of your country or community has changed in recent years.

> *Example*   ***France has tightened its immigration policy in the past year.***

1. _____

2. _____

3. _____

SHIFTING VERB TENSES

Think for a moment about the topic of change. When you write about any change, you are likely to write about a present-day situation and possible future outcomes. In addition, you may also write about past events that affect the present and the future. And, you may write about events that move from the past to the present.

Look at this paragraph about changing a personal habit:

> Whenever I speak English in front of people, I feel nervous. One time, when I was a high school student, I participated in an English speech contest. When I mispronounced the word *school*, I saw a judge laughing at me. Suddenly, my mind was blank, my face turned red, and I forgot what to say. Every

time I speak English, I recall the judge's laughing face. Because of his reaction, I lost a lot of confidence in speaking English. This bad experience has made me depressed ever since then, but I really want to give myself another chance.

Ching Ting Liao
Taiwan

1. Find the sentences in which the student writer uses the present tense. Why does she use this tense?

2. When does the student use the past tense?

3. Why does the student use the present perfect tense in the last sentence?

This writer uses different verb tenses because she discusses different time frames.

Verb Tense	Time Frame
I **feel** nervous.	habitual feeling
I **participated** in an English speech contest.	past event
This bad experience **has made** me depressed.	feeling from the past to the present

This writer shifts verb tenses successfully by keeping the different time frames in mind as she writes. You must do the same when you write about events that took place at different times and that are involved in a change.

Exercise 7.10   In the paragraph that follows, underline the main verbs. Identify the verb tenses, and be prepared to discuss why each verb tense is used.

Modern technology has taken away many jobs. Years ago, my grandfather worked hard in a big company assembling television sets. My grandmother worked in a high school cafeteria selling sodas and pies and biscuits that she had baked. How surprised both of my grandparents would be to know that, in this era, a robot is doing my grandfather's job, and a vending machine is placed where my grandmother used to sell her homemade products. Would they be happy living in this time, resting while machines do their jobs? This is one of the privileges of modern life, which thousands of unemployed workers can now enjoy. These people can now sit in their homes, watching TV and eating biscuits, because machines have taken their jobs.

Jorge Caldas
Colombia

Exercise 7.11   In the following paragraph, notice the italicized verbs. Edit the verb tenses for any inappropriate time shifts. Some of the verbs are correct.

An Important Lesson in My Life

During my thirty years, I *have learned* a lot of things in my life, but an important thing *is to think* positively and *make* everything bright in my life. Before I *came* to the U.S., when I *do* something, I always *think* it *is* impossible, and I *cannot do* it. The reason *is* that when I *was* a student, I *have* a lot of hopes of being successful. But every time I *am* hopeful, in the end I always *lose*. After a while, this *make* me feel upset. However, when I *came* to the U.S., I *meet* a friend who *is* a positive person. When he *does* anything, he always *keeps* his mind open. Whenever I *feel* upset or *lose* hope, he *was* always beside me and *tells* me, "Ling, in everything you *must think* positively. Then, you *can do* it." So now, when I *do* something, I *have thought* about what he *is saying.* "Everything *is* possible."

Ling-Ling Lin
People's Republic of China

GERUNDS AND INFINITIVES

Remember that gerunds and infinitives are commonly used as nouns—as subjects or as objects in sentences.

Look at how gerunds and infinitives are used in these sentences from "Solving the Traffic Problems in Taipei":

S

In Taipei, it is very difficult <u>to find</u> a space for parking.

O

They rush ahead without <u>yielding</u>.

S

Consequently, <u>driving</u> a car in Taipei is dangerous and difficult.

Exercise 7.12   Complete the following sentences with either a gerund or an infinitive phrase.

Example   _____ is a good way to lose weight.

<u>Eating low-fat foods</u> is a good way to lose weight.

It is almost impossible _____.

It is almost impossible <u>to save money</u>.

1. It's important for me _____.

2. It's necessary for my country _____.

3. _____ takes a long time.

4. _____ will give me more confidence.

5. I can improve my pronunciation by _____.

6. My community must make a commitment to _____.

7. By _____, we can reduce waste.

8. It won't be easy _____.

9. It will cost a lot of money _____.

10. We cannot improve campus security without _____.

FRAGMENTS

A sentence must have a subject and a verb, and it must express a complete thought. A fragment is a piece of a sentence that has been punctuated like a complete sentence. The following are the most common causes of fragments:

1. Often the fragment is a subordinate clause or phrase.

   Fragments: **Because I didn't want to stay in Florida.** I decided to change universities and move to Washington, D.C.

   Wanting to improve my reading skills. I have recently started reading novels in English.

   Because I didn't want to stay in Florida is a subordinate clause, and it does not express a complete thought. *Wanting to improve my reading skills* is a participial phrase, a pattern which lacks a subject and verb. Both of these fragments must be attached to a complete sentence like this:

   Complete sentence: **Because I didn't want to stay in Florida,** I decided to change universities and move to Washington, D.C.

   Complete sentence: **Wanting to improve my reading skills,** I have recently started reading novels in English.

2. A fragment may have a missing subject.

   Fragment: *Complete sentence:*

   Is important to do my work.   **It** is important to do my work.

3. A fragment may have a missing verb.

Fragment:

Many teenagers from broken families.

Complete sentence:

Many teenagers **come** from broken families.

4. A fragment may have no subject or verb.

Fragment:

I have made a lot of changes since I came to the U.S. For example, cleaning my house and doing my laundry.

Complete sentence:

I have made a lot of changes since I came to the U.S., for example, cleaning my house and doing my laundry.

or **I have made a lot of changes since I came to the U.S. For example, now I clean my house and do my laundry.**

Exercise 7.13   Find the fragments in the following sentences and correct them. Some of the sentences are complete.

1. Farid decided to change jobs. Since his boss would not give him a pay raise.

2. Whenever I have some troubles. I usually become impatient and feel bored, nervous, and angry.

3. When I get angry, I hit or destroy several things. For example, tape recorders and cars that don't work normally.

4. Although it may be difficult to change. I had better do it.

5. When I change my shortcoming. I will feel better than I do now.

6. I will reward myself for every small improvement. For example, buy myself a record or a new item of clothing.

7. Before we try to solve the problem, we must understand it.

8. My attitude toward studying not like my sister's.

9. Feeling frustrated. I decided to make a change.

Revising

Exchange papers ("A Change in Your Community") with a partner, and read each other's essay. Have your partner consider the questions on the Writing Checklist below.

Writing Checklist

1. Does the essay have an introduction paragraph? Does it have a thesis statement?
2. Does the essay's body follow one of the two outlines suggested on pages 135–136? If so, does each body paragraph have a topic sentence and adequate supporting ideas?
3. Does the essay have a concluding paragraph?
4. Does the writer use appropriate verb tenses?
5. Are there any fragments?

Journal Writing

A. Write one page in your journal on one of these topics:

1. How have you changed since you came to the United States?

2. Change is not always positive, but we often learn from it. Write about a difficult change in your life from which you learned something.

B. Write one page in your journal on a topic of your choice.

More Writing Topics

1. Write an essay about a change that a close friend or family member needs to make.

2. Write an essay about changes that need to be made in the school where you study now.

3. Write an essay based on this statement:

   "Once I thought _____; now I think _____."

Chapter 8

Making Judgments

What are some important choices that you make?

How do you make choices?

What qualities do you consider when you choose a product?

Comparing Places in Your Community

Getting Ideas

PHOTOGRAPHS
Examine the photographs on the previous page to find similarities and differences (top, Honda Civic EX, bottom, Nissan Sentra GXE).

BRAINSTORMING
Read the features of the two automobiles pictured above. With a partner, decide which automobile you prefer, and discuss why.

Honda Civic EX	Nissan Sentra GXE
Price :$14,675 (with options*)	Price: $16,360 (with options*)
Handles well on turns	Handles adequately on turns
Roomy rear seat	Average-sized rear seat
Good, firm ride	Smooth, firm ride
Gas: averages 29 mpg	Gas: averages 28 mpg
Transmission shifts well on hills	Transmission shifts smoothly

*Options on both cars include automatic transmission, air conditioning, and stereo cassette player.

Composing

COMPARISON AND CONTRAST

Comparison and contrast are useful in both your personal and academic life. You make choices each time you compare prices at the supermarket or decide which television show to watch. At your college or university, you may be asked to compare a society before and after an important historical event, to contrast two scientific theories, or to compare two famous persons.

It's natural to make comparisons in many types of writing. When you wrote about a change, in the last chapter, you probably compared your personal life or your community before and after the change. If you wrote about a decision in chapter 3, you may have contrasted how you felt before and after the decision.

In this chapter you are going to explore how to organize a comparison/contrast essay by comparing similar places and products. The organization, structures, and vocabulary that you learn will serve you in a variety of writing situations.

CHOOSING COMPARABLE ITEMS

To begin, any fair comparison requires that the writer choose two comparable, or similar, items to compare. Items are similar when they have similar functions, and, sometimes, features. For instance, would it be fair to compare a Mercedes-Benz 300 with a Ford Escort? What types of cars are comparable?

Exercise 8.1   With a partner, write the names of two comparable examples for each of the groups below. Discuss why your examples can be compared.

1. restaurants in your city

   _____

2. universities

   _____

3. musical groups

   _____

4. TV shows

   _____

5. stores

BASES OF COMPARISON

Look again at the features of the two cars on page 153 of this chapter. Can you put the features into three logical groups?

You could put the features of the automobiles into basic groups such as economy, comfort and convenience, and performance.

These three groups could form the bases for comparison that a writer might use to compare the two automobiles. Using bases of comparison facilitates the organization of the essay, allowing the writer and the reader to see clearly what aspects of the two items will be compared.

When a writer compares two items, he or she must compare the same aspects of each item. For example, a writer cannot fairly compare a Mazda 626 with a Honda Civic by describing only the Mazda's economy and only the Honda's convenience. The writer should discuss the same aspects of both automobiles.

Exercise 8.2   With your class, think of fast-food restaurants, such as McDonald's or Burger King. Brainstorm a list of possibly comparable restaurants, and write their names on the chalkboard. Discuss which fast-food restaurants are comparable. Then, as a class, choose two of them that most of the class is familiar with.

Brainstorm a list of features of each restaurant on the board, and copy the features onto the chart below. One example feature is given.

Fast-Food Restaurant A Name:	Fast-Food Restaurant B Name:
drive-through window	

Exercise 8.3   Next, examine the list, and group the related features into three general areas. For example, several features may be grouped under Food Quality. Discard any features that don't fall into one of your three categories. These groups will be the bases of comparison.

```
┌─────────────────────────────────────────────────────────┐
│         Bases of Comparison and Supporting Features       │
│                                                           │
│   1. Food Quality          2. _____    3. _____ │
│      Fresh Salad                                          │
│                                                           │
│                                                           │
│                                                           │
│                                                           │
│                                                           │
│                                                           │
└─────────────────────────────────────────────────────────┘
```

THESIS STATEMENT: COMPARISON/CONTRAST ESSAY

Why would someone want to write a comparison of two automobiles? Why would a person compare two restaurants in writing?

In comparison/contrast writing, the purposes for writing vary. A writer might present his or her comparison to show that one item is superior to the other. Other reasons might be to simply say that the two items are basically alike or that they have surprising differences.

For Writing Assignment 1: Comparing Places in Your Community, your purpose will be to give your dominant impression of two comparable places to members of your writing class.

Your thesis statement should include the names of the two places being compared as well as your dominant impression about the places.

Example thesis statement: **Burger King is as good a choice for a quick meal as McDonald's because of food, service, and value.**

Exercise 8.4

1. Using the information on page 153, write a thesis statement for an essay in which you compare the Honda Civic EX and the Nissan Sentra GXE.

2. Write a thesis statement for an essay in which you compare two comparable universities.

OUTLINING A COMPARISON/CONTRAST ESSAY

To organize your writing for Writing Assignment 1, use the sample outline below. It presents an outline for an essay comparing the Honda Civic EX with the Nissan Sentra GXE.

I. Introduction
    A. State the function of each item.
    B. Establish the reason for the comparison/contrast.

C. Thesis statement: State your dominant impression about the two items. (The dominant impression could be that they are basically alike, that one is superior, that they have surprising differences, or that they have some differences and some similarities.)

Example thesis statement: **The Honda Civic EX is generally the same as the Nissan Sentra GXE in economy, performance, and comfort.**

II. Body paragraph I: Compare the two cars in terms of economy.

Example topic sentence: **In terms of economy, the Honda and the Nissan are comparable.**

A. Honda Civic EX
   1. Cost of car
   2. Miles per gallon (mpg)
B. Nissan Sentra GXE
   1. Cost of car
   2. Miles per gallon (mpg)

III. Body paragraph II: Compare the two cars in terms of performance.

Example topic sentence: **In addition, the Honda Civic and the Nissan Sentra perform equally well.**

A. Honda Civic EX
   1. Handling
   2. Transmission
B. Nissan Sentra GXE
   1. Handling
   2. Transmission

IV. Body paragraph III: Compare the two cars in terms of comfort.

Example topic sentence: **Finally, the Honda Civic and the Nissan Sentra offer similar comfort.**

A. Honda Civic EX
   1. Ride
   2. Rear seat
B. Nissan Sentra GXE
   1. Ride
   2. Rear seat

V. Conclusion

A. Restate the thesis statement: Give your dominant impression of the two cars.
B. If you can, recommend which car to buy.

Exercise 8.5 Write a practice outline for a comparison/contrast essay about the two fast-food restaurants which your class selected in Exercise 8.2.

MAKING LOGICAL CONNECTIONS IN THE INTRODUCTION

Read the introductory paragraph on the top of page 159. Look again at the outline presented on page 157 and this page. Find the sentences in the introduction that contain information suggested in the outline.

McDonald's Versus Burger King

McDonald's and Burger King are probably the two largest fast-food chains in the United States. No matter where you live, you can almost certainly find one or both of these franchises in your neighborhood. But should you drive the extra miles needed to go to one rather than the other? Since McDonald's and Burger King offer basically the same food, atmosphere, and service, it doesn't really matter where you stop to eat.

This introduction of a comparison/contrast essay contains the elements suggested in the outline. The first sentence introduces the two items being compared and defines their function as "fast food chains." The next two sentences state the reason for the comparison: to explain whether someone should choose one restaurant over the other. Finally, the last sentence answers this question, stating that both places "offer basically the same food, atmosphere, and service . . .". The thesis statement includes the three bases of comparison that will appear in the essay.

The sentences in the introductory paragraph create a logical chain in which each sentence leads clearly to the next.

Look at the introduction again. The underlined words and arrows indicate the logical connections made by referring to previous ideas.

McDonald's and Burger King are two of the largest fast-food chains in the United States.

No matter where you live, you can almost certainly find one or both of these franchises in your neighborhood.

But should you drive the extra miles needed to go to one rather than the other?

Since McDonald's and Burger King offer basically the same food, atmosphere, and service, it doesn't really matter where you stop to eat.

Exercise 8.6   Read the introduction below. In each sentence after the first sentence, underline words or phrases that connect to the previous ideas.

The Honda Civic EX and the Nissan GXE are both popular Japanese cars in the United States. If you want to buy a new Japanese car, which one will you choose? It is hard to make a decision. However, there are few differences between these two cars in the areas of economy, technical performance, and convenience. Because of their similarities, you will find that either car is a good choice.

Exercise 8.7   Each of the introductory paragraphs that follow contains a logical gap. In other words, there is a jump between ideas that needs to be bridged by the writer. Add a sentence or sentences that would make the ideas in the paragraph connect logically.

1. The most important piece of equipment for a runner is shoes. Choosing the right pair of running shoes can make all the difference in how well a person runs. There are hundreds of kinds of running shoes available. _____

   _____

   Because they give more support, more comfort, and better value, the Pike Runners are better than the Nubok Flyers.

2. As I was deciding to buy a personal computer, a colleague advised me that "the Morris is your best friend, and the Olympic is your worst enemy." _____

   _____

   I chose the Olympic because it was cheaper, faster, and more versatile.

3. The Honda Civic and Nissan Sentra are mid-sized cars in the United States. They have some good features that big American cars don't have. _____

   _____

   Therefore, you can buy either one.

Exercise 8.8   Write an introduction for an essay that compares the Honda Civic EX with the Nissan Sentra GXE. Be sure that your introduction contains the elements suggested in the outline and that each sentence connects logically with the previous sentence.

Writing

For Writing Assignment 1, you will evaluate two comparable places in your community. Your audience will be this class. Your purpose will be to inform consumers about two places they may be considering visiting. You may conclude that one of the places is better, that they are basically alike or very different, or that they share similarities and differences.

Here are some tasks to help you get started:

1. First, select two comparable places to evaluate. (Remember that *comparable* means similar in function.) Choose places that you are familiar with and which you can visit, so that you will be able to *compare and contrast* them with authority.

Examples	**two hamburger joints**	**two supermarkets**
	two pizza parlors	**two universities**
	two convenience stores	**two fitness centers**
	two video stores	**two music stores**

2. Go to your chosen places and observe them. Take notes about what you see, hear, smell, and feel. Be as detailed as possible in your note taking, but concentrate on the features

that impress you the most. As soon as you get home, make a list of the outstanding features of each place. Include the ways in which the two places are similar and different.

3. On the assigned day, come to class with your notes on the places and the list of features.

4. Organize your notes into an outline that includes the bases for your comparison.

5. After the teacher or a classmate has checked your outline, write your essay.

Building Language Skills

COMPARATIVE FORMS

English has many patterns for comparing items.

1. You can show equality between two items:

The Honda Civic looks as beautiful as the Nissan Sentra.

The workers at McDonald's work as diligently as the workers at Burger King.

The Honda Civic gets about the same gas mileage as the Nissan Sentra.

2. You can show inequality between two items:

The Ford Escort has a smaller rear seat than the Ford Taurus.

A Jaguar is more expensive than a Peugeot.

Most pick-up trucks are less comfortable than most vans.

My new car's transmission performs more smoothly than my old car's.

The following are simplified charts of these two types of comparative patterns.

COMPARATIVES OF EQUALITY			
Adjective	as	comfortable	as
Adverb	as	quickly	as
Noun	the same	size	as

COMPARATIVES OF INEQUALITY			
	One syllable	**Two syllables**	
Adjective	smaller	more expensive	than
Adverb	faster	less smoothly	than
Plural count nouns	more doors fewer doors		than
Noncount nouns	more fuel less fuel		than

Some irregular comparative forms exist.

Examples   In my view, a four-door car is **better than** a two-door car.

My old car runs **worse than** my new car.

Refer to your grammar textbook for a more thorough review of the rules and the irregular patterns of comparative forms of adjectives, adverbs, and nouns.

Exercise 8.9   Look at the following menus of two coffee bars, and write ten sentences, using comparative forms.

Examples   **Café Blanc serves fewer items than Café Noir.**

The capuccino is cheaper at Café Blanc than at Café Noir.

Café Blanc
Cappuccino $2.00
Café Latte $2.00
Espresso $2.00
Mocha Java $1.25
Muffins $1.00
Cake $1.75
Biscotti $1.00
Hours 7 A.M. to 11 P.M. Monday–Saturday 10 A.M. to 6 P.M. Sunday

Café Noir
Cappuccino $2.50
Café Latte $2.50
Espresso $2.00
Mocha Java $1.50
French-Pressed Coffee $1.75
Iced Coffee $1.25
Muffins $1.00
Cake $1.75
Biscotti $1.00
Hours 8 A.M. to 10 P.M. Monday–Saturday Closed Sunday

TRANSITIONS FOR COMPARISON AND CONTRAST

In addition to comparative forms, other types of transitions can indicate when items are similar or different.

In the paragraph below, the underlined words and phrases show similarities and differences between one aspect of the two coffee bars.

One difference between the two coffee bars is price. At Café Blanc, the prices are generally lower than at Café Noir. For example, the cappuccino and the café latte at Café Blanc cost only $2.00 each, whereas at Café Noir, the two items cost $2.50 each. You can get a cup of mocha java at Café Blanc for $1.25, but at Café Noir, it's $1.50. On the other hand, a few items cost the same at both places. The muffins and the biscotti are the same price ($1.00 each) at both cafés. In general, however, Café Blanc has better prices than Café Noir.

TRANSITIONS FOR COMPARISON AND CONTRAST			
Subordinators	**Phrases**	**Transitional Expressions**	**Conjunctions**
whereas while	unlike different from	on the other hand in contrast however	but yet
	like similar to	in the same way similarly likewise	and

The sentences that follow show how each type of transition is used with different sentence patterns and different punctuation.

1. Subordinators:

   While the Nissan Sentra costs $16,360, the Honda Civic EX costs only $14,675.

2. Phrases:

   Unlike a sports car, a sedan has a roomy rear seat.

3. Transitional Expressions:

   Small cars are economical on gasoline; on the other hand, large cars aren't.

4. Conjunctions:

   The Honda gets 29 miles per gallon, but the Nissan averages only 28.

Exercise 8.10   In the paragraphs below, add appropriate transitions in the blanks. Not all show comparison and contrast.

The way we dress when dating in a formal or casual way differs. On a formal date, a couple usually is well dressed. They wear their favorite, pretty, and, maybe, expensive clothes. Usually, the male wears a jacket, a long-sleeve shirt, and a tie. _In the same way_, the lady takes special care in the way she looks and wears high heels and possibly a skirt. _____Furthermore_____ (Also), she uses more makeup than she normally does. ___On the other hand___, on a casual date, a couple can wear jeans or shorts and sneakers. The girl doesn't wear much makeup and looks more natural. Of course, dressing takes less time on a casual date than on a formal date.

Also, we behave differently on each kind of date. Having a formal date implies that we have to be more respectful: men have to be "gentlemen" and women "ladies." For instance, a man should pick the lady up at her house, open the car door for her, drive carefully, and pay the bills. In other words, a man has to be a "good boy." ___Likewise___, the woman should be polite and attentive. ___Unlike___ a formal date, a casual date is more relaxed because the man and the woman are more natural in the way that they talk and behave without any restrictions of conduct. For example, on a casual date, it is more likely they will go "dutch," to make different kinds of jokes, and to laugh loudly. Little mistakes can be easily forgotten, such as not opening the car door or forgetting the credit card. Going on a formal date requires more careful behavior, ___but___ a casual date is more relaxed.

Daniel Beuses
Venezuela

Revising

Read your partner's essay comparing places in your community for content and organization. Consider the following questions. Make notes in the margins where you see content or organization problems related to these questions. Discuss them with your partner.

Writing Checklist

1. Does the essay's introductory paragraph contain the elements suggested in the outline? Does it tell the function of the two places? That is, does it present a reason for the comparison? Does it contain a thesis statement that gives the writer's dominant impression of the two places being compared?

2. Does each body paragraph contain a topic sentence which follows the suggested outline? Does each body paragraph compare the same aspects of both places?

3. Does the conclusion restate the thesis statement?

4. Is the essay interesting? Why or why not?

5. Are appropriate transitions for comparison and contrast used?

WRITING ASSIGNMENT 2

Making an Informed Choice

Getting Ideas

BRAINSTORMING

For this assignment, you will have an open topic. You will be asked to compare and contrast any two comparable items or services. To begin, think of products you have recently purchased or that you are going to purchase. For instance, you may want to buy a TV set or a CD player. Perhaps you recently bought a computer. Also, think of services you have recently selected or are going to select. Some of you may have chosen an apartment or a long-distance telephone company before you joined this class. Or you may select a college or a university in the near future.

Brainstorm topics for this essay with your class. Select topics that are broad enough to write about in a four- or five-paragraph essay.

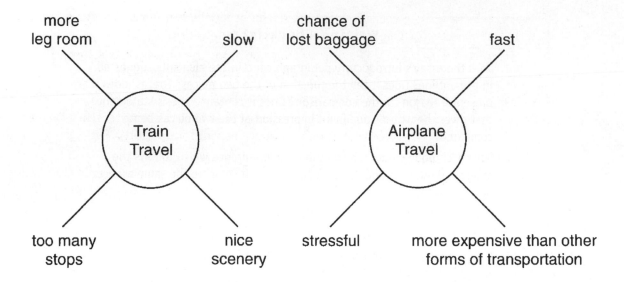

CLUSTERING

When you have a topic in mind, jot down ideas for your essay by using a cluster drawing. In the center of each cluster, write each item you will compare. Write important features of each item around the center of the cluster. Use the drawing above as a guide. If you do not have enough information for your essay, you may need to do some research into the two products or services you will compare.

BASES OF COMPARISON

Next, examine the features you wrote for each item. Group the features into three categories. Use the same three categories for each item. Discard any features that do not fit into your categories. These categories will be the three bases of comparison for your essay.

Composing

OUTLINING

On pages 157-158 you were introduced to a method of organizing a comparison essay in which each basis of comparison is presented in a separate paragraph. Another way to organize a comparison essay is to present each item and its features in a separate paragraph, as in the outline that follows.

I.   Introduction

   A.   State the function of each item.

   B.   Establish the reason for the comparison/contrast.

C. Thesis statement: State your dominant impression about the two items. (In this essay, the dominant impression will be that one item is superior to the other.)

Example thesis statement: **For the average person, the Olympic is a better personal computer than the Morris.**

II. Body Paragraph I: Present Item 1 and the bases of comparison.

Example topic sentence: **The Morris compares less favorably with the Olympic in terms of value, speed, and versatility.**

A. Basis 1 + details

B. Basis 2 + details

C. Basis 3 + details

III. Body paragraph II: Present Item 2 and refer to the features being evaluated.

Example topic sentence: **In contrast, the Olympic surpasses the Morris in value, speed, and versatility.**

A. Basis 1 + details

B. Basis 2 + details

C. Basis 3 + details

IV. Conclusion

A. Restate the thesis statement: Give your dominant impression of the two items.

B. Recommend which one to buy.

Write an outline of your essay, "Making an Informed Choice," using whichever outline format is best suited to your topic.

COHERENCE: REPETITION OF KEY IDEAS

In chapter 3, you learned that ordering your ideas and using transition words are important ways to make your writing smooth and coherent. In chapter 5, you saw how using pronouns to refer to earlier ideas also adds coherence.

Yet another way to make your writing smooth is by repeating key ideas. You can do this by repeating key words or by using synonymous phrases.

Read the following paragraph, in which key ideas are underlined.

The two restaurants differ considerably in atmosphere. Fu's Garden is elegant and calm. The restaurant has classy jade carvings on its walls. The tables are made of rich mahogany wood. They are covered with pale pink tablecloths, which gives the place a feeling of tranquility. The pink color scheme is echoed in the chair seats and wall trim. All in all, it is an elegant and restful place to have dinner. The Golden Bowl, on the other hand, has a bright and busy atmosphere. Its wall decorations are shiny brass letters and gongs. The simple white tables are brightened by red tablecloths, and red paper lanterns hang throughout the restaurant. These colors give it a lively feeling.

Key words are repeated to reinforce the main idea of the paragraph. The first restaurant has a calm and elegant atmosphere, and the second restaurant is bright and busy.

● **Exercise 8.11**   In the paragraph on the next page, underline the key words and synonymous phrases that make this paragraph coherent.

A Journey to the Caspian Sea

The north of Iran is more marvelous than other areas because it lies beside the Caspian Sea. Almost all Iranians spend a few days of their summer vacation in the north of Iran. The road to the north is mountainous. The highest mountain in Iran, Damavand, stands in this part of Iran, too. But many people prefer to drive by car because beyond these mountains you have a wonderful view of the sea. In fact, the road was made between the sea and the forest. The sunset at the seaside of the Caspian Sea is very dramatic. At this time, many people like to sit on the beach to wait for the moment when the yellow and red sky joins the blue sea. The mountains, the winding road, the sea—all these make this one of the most spectacular areas of my country.

Anahita Tavakoli
Iran

CONCLUSION: RECOMMENDATION

In chapter 7, you learned that the conclusion paragraph is an essential part of an essay. It not only reiterates the writer's main point, but it can also include other information, such as a result or a prediction, depending on the type of essay.

In a comparison essay, it's often logical to make a recommendation in the conclusion. If you decide, for instance, that one car is better than another, you can recommend that the reader buy the one you recommend. In addition, you may summarize the main points of the essay.

Exercise 8.12 Read the essay that follows. Add a logical conclusion paragraph that presents a recommendation to the reader.

The Differences Between Nikos-Nikos and Andros Restaurants

Nikos-Nikos and Andros are two well-known Greek restaurants in Houston. Both of these restaurants are medium-sized and inexpensive. Although the two restaurants are similar, I can distinguish some differences in their convenience, environment, and variety of food that make me prefer Andros.

Nikos-Nikos, a popular Greek restaurant, is located at Westheimer and Montrose streets. It is very easy for everybody in Houston to get there, especially for people who work near downtown. Easy access is important for people who want to eat Greek food without spending much time. On the other hand, Andros is located at Fondren Road and Westpark Street, which is far away from downtown and from all the city's main business areas. It is not very convenient for business people. For example, if I am working downtown and I have one hour for lunch, I prefer to go to Nikos-Nikos rather than Andros because it will take me only fifteen minutes to get there and fifteen minutes to come back. In short, Nikos-Nikos is more convenient than Andros because of the location.

Although Andros is not as convenient as Nikos-Nikos, Andros has two advantages that Nikos-Nikos doesn't. The first advantage is the environment. Andros has a better environment and a more friendly atmosphere. Andros gives you the sensation that you are in a real Greek restaurant. The family that owns the place and works there is Greek. They are dressed in traditional Greek clothing and they speak Greek. Also, the interior of Andros is decorated with beautiful pictures of Greece. Further, the waiters are very friendly. They serve the customers with smiles and with helpful advice. On the other hand, Nikos-Nikos doesn't have such a pleasant atmosphere because non-Greek people are working there, and they are not accustomed to Greek customs. In my opinion, if you want to have a traditional restaurant, you have to exhibit the customs of the country. This is the reason why Andros has a better environment than Nikos-Nikos.

Another advantage that Andros has is the variety of food. The variety of food is one of the first things that a customer notices when he or she goes to a restaurant. Andros has a large selection of traditional Greek food. There are many appetizers, vegetable and meat courses, and desserts. In contrast, Nikos-Nikos doesn't have a big variety. It is more of a fast-food restaurant, where you can find only five basic kinds of Greek food, such as gyros and spinach pies. I prefer Andros to Nikos-Nikos because it has a larger menu. I have been a customer at these places several times, but because I like to eat something different each time, Andros is the place that suits me better.

Argyris Kafantaris
Greece

In conclusion, _____

_____

_____

_____

Note: The authors omitted the conclusion paragraph of the essay for this exercise.

Writing

Use your outline and the information you have learned in this chapter to write an essay in which you compare and contrast two products or services that you have chosen or will choose in the future. Include a recommendation to the reader about which one is superior.

Building Language Skills

VOCABULARY: WORD FORMS

Choosing the correct form of a word to say what you want to say is important. You may, for instance, want to express the idea of "different," but this idea takes many forms in English: you may use an adjective *different*, a verb, *differ;* a noun, *difference;* or an adverb, *differently.* As the sentences that follow illustrate, you must consider the particular function of a word in choosing which form to use:

> Seattle and Denver are very **different** cities.

> First, they **differ** considerably in climate.

> Another major **difference** between the two cities is the pace of life.

> Finally, Seattle and Denver residents act **differently** toward foreigners.

Exercise 8.13   Correct the sentences below, which contain errors in word forms. Write your revision below each original sentence.

> *Example*   **My friend is dynamic and sincerity.**
>
> *My friend is dynamic and sincere.*

1. The movie had many excited scenes.

2. The pollution is visibly.

3. Many women wonder what the idealist job is for them.

4. I like to see the happy of children.

5. Living alone made me grow up and experienced.

6. The only job that can make my dream come true is to becoming the President of the United States.

7. I am very well at playing basketball.

8. This car has as much powerful as the other one.

9. The tuition fees are extreme high.

10. Most people are concern about crime.

VERB FORMS

Using verbs appropriately in English is a challenge in writing. Once you have established the time frame, you must know how to form the verb tense correctly.

Look at the sentences below, which illustrate the common problems that can occur in using verb forms in writing:

Some students are study hard.

I have learn about different cultures in my class.

The teacher never come to class on time.

With your class, correct the errors in these sentences.

Exercise 8.14 Correct the verb-form errors in the following sentences. Make your corrections above each line.

1. The beach have white sand and is surrounded by mountains.

2. In the past ten years, tennis has becoming a popular sport for three reasons.

3. If teachers always go to class on time and they don't absent, students usually follow the teacher's example.

4. Both males and females know how to choose a mate who really suit them.

5. In the past, marriages were arrange by their parents or someone else.

6. I was not expected the gift that I received.

7. The computer was become a part of my life.

8. The change was happened slowly.

Revising

Have a partner read over your essay, "Making an Informed Choice," and suggest revisions, using the Writing Checklist below as a guide. Then, revise your essay accordingly.

Journal Writing

A.   Write a one-page entry in your journal on one of the following topics:

 1. Write about a product or service that you have chosen incorrectly.

 2. Write about a time in your life when someone helped you make an important judgment.

B.   Write a one-page entry on a topic of your choice.

More Writing Topics

1.   Compare two friends that you know well, or compare two siblings.

2.   Compare two of your favorite cities.

3.   Compare college life with high school life.

Chapter 9

The Order of Things

What kinds of classmates do you have?

What are some characteristics that distinguish your teachers?

Classifying Members of Your Community

Getting Ideas

READING

After reading the following essay, discuss the questions below with your classmates.

Our Class's Relationship with Teachers

Many students think school is a boring and unnecessary place, while other students find school instructive and interesting. Students have different attitudes toward school and their teachers. Almost all of the students in our class can be classified according to their relationship with teachers.

The first category includes students who are in opposition to the teacher. These students always raise their voices as soon as the teacher mentions something about homework or, even worse, a test. They try to convince the teacher that homework or a test is not a good idea. These students think that teachers must have been put on earth just to make students' lives terrible. Therefore, they have to argue with the teacher. An excellent example of a student who is in opposition to the teacher is Woody. This student strongly believes that teachers are the worst people living on earth. He always has something to object to when it comes to homework, and he challenges the teacher when she wants to give a test.

The second category includes students who are intimidated by the teacher. These students are often very shy and like to sit in the back row of the classroom. Sitting far away from the teacher makes them feel a little bit safer. What they really want to do is to run away and hide somewhere where they don't need to answer any questions. These students whisper when they have to talk, and they wouldn't even think of asking the teacher a question. What if the teacher thinks it's a stupid question and starts to laugh? A good example of a student who is intimidated is Jiamin. She sits in the back row, trying to hide from the teacher. When the teacher tells her to read aloud from the grammar book, she whispers a few sentences in a tiny voice and then stops.

The last and most common category in our class includes students who are relaxed with the teacher. These students talk, laugh, and ask the teacher for help. They don't have to argue with or hide from the teacher, like the students in the first and second category. These students take the teacher for what he or she really is: a person who is there to help the students as much as possible. These students also understand that if you talk with the teacher and show him that you are interested and want to learn English, he will help you achieve that goal. Thanasis and Carlos are good examples of students who are relaxed with the teacher. Before and after class, they talk to the teacher about their personal lives or about anything that is on their minds. They never hesitate to ask the teacher for advice or help, and they like to help him in any way they can.

There are, of course, many more categories of students, but in our class the students who are in opposition to the teacher, intimidated by the teacher, or relaxed with the teacher are the most significant categories. As a student, you spend so much time in a classroom, with different teachers, that you should try to build a good relationship with your teachers. If you are relaxed and treat a teacher as a "friend," he or she can help you to make the time you have to spend in school more comfortable.

Cecilia Rickardsson
Sweden

•Discussion:

1. What is the writer trying to do in this essay?

2. What is the thesis statement?

3. How does the writer classify the students?

4. How does the writer define the first category of students? What are the characteristics of the first group? How does the writer define the second category? What are the characteristics of the second group? How does the writer define the third category? What are the characteristics of the third group?

5. Does the writer use appropriate examples to illustrate the categories?

6. Can you substitute members of your class into each of the categories?

Composing

CLASSIFICATION ESSAY: PRINCIPLE OF CLASSIFICATION

The pattern of writing used in "Our Class's Relationship with Teachers" is called classification. This pattern is used to analyze a topic by dividing it into groups whose members share common characteristics. The purpose of doing this is to learn something about a topic, such as a class, by breaking it down into smaller groups.

The writer of "Our Class's Relationship with Teachers" separates the topic of students into three categories: those who are in opposition to the teacher, those who are intimidated by the teacher, and those who are relaxed with the teacher.

The writer divides the students on the basis of their relationship with their teachers, so this is her principle of classification.

What are some other ways you could classify students? Fill in the blanks with your ideas.

Students can be classified **according to   their nationality.**

according to _____.

_____.

_____.

Each of those ways of looking at students represents a different principle of classification.

When you classify, you choose the principle of classification. But you should use only one principle of classification. For example, you could classify jobs on the basis of level of stress *or* on the basis of salary; however, you should not divide jobs into those that are high stress, those that are low stress, and those that pay over $50,000. If you did, you would be using two principles of classification.

Exercise 9.1   The topics below have been divided into several categories. Read the topics and categories and discuss what principle of classification has been used to divide the topics.

Topic: **Teachers: easy-going; strict; moderately strict**
   Principle of classification: level of discipline

1. Topic: Clothing: sportswear; formal wear; professional clothes
   Principle of classification: ___level of dress___

2. Topic: Friends: those you see every day; those you see once a month; those you see once a year

   Principle of classification: ___level of closeness___

3. Topic: Leisure activities: with family; with friends; by myself

   Principle of classification: ___level of involvement___

4. Topics: Jobs: those that require minimal education; those that require a bachelor's degree; those that require extensive education

   Principle of classification: ___level of education___

5. Topic: Computer software: entertaining; educational; practical
   Principle of classification: ___level of kind use___

6. Topic: American cars: Ford; Chevrolet; Oldsmobile
   Principle of classification: ___level of price___

7. Topic: Regions: desert; savanna; rain forest
   Principle of classification: ___level of rain___

Exercise 9.2 Examine the cluster diagrams that follow, each of which divides a class into several categories. Determine the principle of classification that is used. Find the category that doesn't belong.

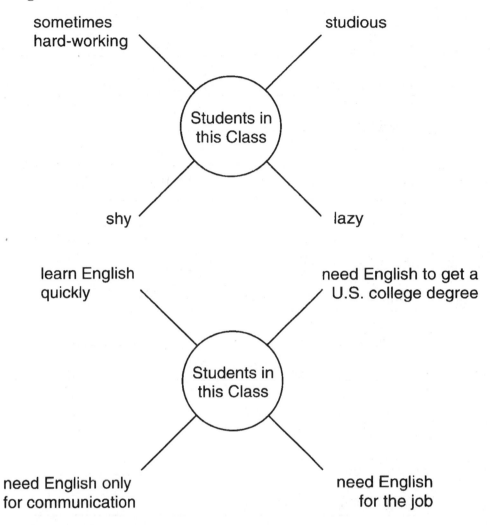

sometimes
hard-working

studious

Students in
this Class

shy

lazy

learn English
quickly

need English to get a
U.S. college degree

Students in
this Class

need English only
for communication

need English
for the job

Exercise 9.3 For each classification, look at the topic and the one category given. Identify the principle of classification. Then, add two more categories that belong in this classification.

Example   **Topic: Movies**
Principle of classification: _____

Categories: *movies that have no violence or almost none*

_____

_____

Topic: Movies
Principle of classification: *amount of violence*

Categories: *movies that have no violence or almost none*
movies that have a moderate amount of violence
movies that have extreme violence

1. Topic: Cars

   Principle of classification: ___level of prices___

   Categories: *economy cars* _____

   moderate cars

   expensive cars

   extreme expensive cars = luxury

2. Topic: Movies

   Principle of classification: ___movies rating___

   Categories: *G-rated* _____

   P. G. rated

   AA .

   _____

3. Topic: Teachers

   Principle of classification: ___level of education___

   Categories: *those with bachelor's degrees* _____

   those with major's degrees

   M.A. Master busness   those with master's degrees
   fine art   philosophy   M. A.
   /M. F. A   /   those with speciality's degrees
   Doctor's Ph D— 4 years more

BRAINSTORMING

With your class or a small group, brainstorm the topic of students in your class. Think about all the members in your class. How can you divide them? Try to generate interesting ways to look at the class. What is a principle of classification which you might use?

Next, do the same, using your teachers as the topic.

KEEPING CATEGORIES DISTINCT

Now that you have some ideas about how to classify students or teachers, you need to think about the categories. The categories must obviously fit into the principle of classification, and they must be distinct.

Look back at the sample essay, "Our Class's Relationship with Teachers." The topic was students, and the principle of classification was their relationship with teachers. The writer shows three distinct groups to complete her classification: students who are in opposition to the teacher, students who are intimidated by the teacher, and students who are relaxed with the teacher.

Each of these categories is clearly separate from the others. If the writer had used the categories "students who are relaxed with the teacher" and "students who are friendly with the teacher," then these two categories would have overlapped, and they would not have been distinct.

ORGANIZING

Write a sentence that presents the group you are classifying (students in your class) and the principle of classification. Follow this model to construct your sentence:

Example   **Students in my class can be divided according to _____.**

Now, write a sentence that identifies each category. Follow this model:

Example   **The first category is students who _____.**

Next, share your sentences with a partner. Make sure each category fits the principle of classification and that each category is distinct.

OUTLINING A CLASSIFICATION ESSAY

•**Exercise 9.4**   Prepare an outline for Writing Assignment 1 on page 174, a classification of teachers or students. Your thesis statement will be the sentence you wrote earlier that presents your topic and principle of classification. The topic sentences of each body paragraph will be the sentences you wrote to identify each category in your classification. Include the following points in your outline:

I.   Introduction: Identify the topic (group) which you will classify.
Thesis statement: Introduce the classification.

Example thesis statement: **Students in my class can be classified according to the way they dress.**

II.   Topic Sentence: Identify the first category.

Example topic sentence: **The first group consists of students who are trying to make a fashion statement with their clothes.**

   A.   Describe or define the category. What are the general characteristics of the members of this category? Discuss the common characteristics of the members.

   B.   Give examples.

III.   Topic Sentence: Identify the second category.

Example topic sentence: **The next category includes students that are quite eccentric in their dress.**

A. Describe or define the category. What are the general characteristics of the members of this category? Discuss the common characteristics of the members. How is this category different from the first category?

B. Give examples.

IV. Topic Sentence: Identify the third category.

Example topic sentence: **The last group is made up of students who dress in comfortable clothes.**

A. Describe or define the category. What are the general characteristics of the members of this category? Discuss the common characteristics of the members. How is this category different from the first and second categories?

B. Give examples.

V. Conclusion: Restate the thesis statement. Evaluate the categories. Make a personal comment about them.

DEFINING/DESCRIBING CATEGORIES

Once you have established or identified the categories, it's important to define and describe them. What are the characteristics of each category?

In "Our Class's Relationship with Teachers," the writer describes students who are in opposition to the teacher. What do these students do?

It's also important to give one or two examples of typical members of the group. The writer of "Our Class's Relationship with Teachers" does this by naming a class member and describing his or her typical behavior to show the characteristics of the group.

Exercise 9.5: Take one of the categories from the outline you prepared earlier for this writing assignment. Begin with the topic sentence you wrote earlier. Then add sentences that would describe the characteristics of the category. Next, add example(s) of typical members of the group and describe their behavior. Have the teacher or a classmate read your paragraph and check it for coherence.

Writing

After you have prepared an appropriate outline, write your essay. Be sure that you have a single principle of classification, a thesis which introduces the classification, well-defined groups, and examples for each category. Make sure that your readers understand how you have grouped students or teachers by defining the groups adequately and by naming persons who fit into each group.

ADJECTIVE CLAUSES

In the topic sentences of your essay, you will identify each category. To do this, you need to give the distiguishing feature of the category. Look at the following topic sentence:

The first category of vans includes <u>domestic</u> vans.

The adjective <u>domestic</u> tells what kind of vans fall into this category.

Another way to phrase the topic sentence is like this:

The first category includes vans <u>that are made in the United States.</u>

The clause *that are made in the United States* describes the kind of vans in the category. This is called an adjective clause because, like an adjective, it describes a noun.

Adjective clauses are useful structures for defining or describing nouns.

One approach to understanding the formation of adjective clauses is to combine sentences. Look at the following examples:

1.   S

The first category includes vans. The vans are made in the United States.

The first category includes vans **that** are made in the United States.
                          which
                               S

In the new sentence, the relative pronoun *that* is the subject of the adjective clause, replacing the subject, *vans*, in the original sentence. The relative pronouns *that* or *which* can be used to refer to a thing. The adjective clause is placed immediately after the noun it modifies.

2.   S

The first group is teachers. The teachers are easy-going.

The first group is teachers **that** are easy-going.
                  who
                       S

Here the relative pronoun *that* stands for the subject, *teachers*. When a relative pronoun refers to a person in the subject position, you can use *who* or *that*.

3.   S   V   O

One type of friends are friends. You see these friends every day.

One type of friends are friends **that** you see every day.
                        whom
                        who
                        (   )
                         O   S   V

The relative pronoun replaces the object, *these friends,* in the original sentence. When you refer to people in the object position, you can use the pronoun *that, whom,* or *who.* You can also omit the pronoun completely. Remember that the adjective clause comes after the noun it is modifying and that the relative pronoun is moved to the beginning of the clause.

Exercise 9.6 To practice forming adjective clauses, answer the following questions, using an adjective clause to tell what kinds of things you like.

> *Example*   **What kind of people do you like?**
> *I like people who are open-minded and generous.*

1. What kind of clothes do you like? _____

2. What kind of food do you like? _____

3. What kind of teachers do you prefer? _____

4. What kind of homework do you prefer? _____

5. What kind of a partner do you want? _____

Exercise 9.7 The phrases below identify possible categories in a classification of movies. One topic sentence is given to define or describe the category. Write each topic sentence in another way by including an adjective clause in your sentence.

> *Example*   **comic movies**
> **The first group includes comic movies.**
> *The first group includes movies that make you laugh.*

1. horror movies
   The first group includes horror movies.

   _____

2. romantic movies
   The first category is romantic movies.

   _____

3. dramatic movies
   Dramatic movies are the first type of movies.

   _____

4. fantasy movies
   Fantasy movies are the first kind of movies.

   _____

5. animated movies
   The first group of movies includes animated movies.

TRANSITIONS FOR CLASSIFICATION

In your classification essay, you need several types of transition words. Some of these are listed below.

1. Words to introduce categories:

one	first	second	in addition
the next	the last	third	besides

   Example   **One group consists of friends who are casual friends.**

2. Words to contrast categories:

unlike	different from	whereas	while	in contrast to

   Example   **Different from casual friends, "true blue" friends are those one can always count on.**

3. Words to introduce examples:

one example	a good example

   Example   **A good example of a "true blue" friend is my old friend Susan.**

Exercise 9.8   Look at this student paragraph about suspense movies. Underline the transitions used.

Besides horror movies, I also like to see suspense movies. Unlike horror movies, suspense movies seldom have cruel scenes. Many suspense movies have a tricky plot. The directors of these thrillers often use tricky ways to describe the story. We have to pay attention while watching these movies or we won't understand them clearly. Sometimes, suspense movies have strange endings which leave a large space for us to imagine. A good example of a thriller movie that I like very much is "The Hand that Rocks the Cradle." In that movie, we don't know what happens until the movie ends. The director wants to give us wrong clues to find the answer. If we follow the director's clues, we will find a surprising ending. Suspense movies often bring us unpredictable endings.

Pei-Yin Tsai
Taiwan

Revising

Have a partner read your essay for Writing Assignment 1. Then ask your partner to evaluate it for organization. Consider the questions in the Writing Checklist that follows.

Writing Checklist

1. Does the essay contain a thesis statement that presents the topic and the principle of classification?
2. Do the categories follow the principle of classification logically?
3. Does the writer describe the characteristics of each category?
4. Are there examples in each paragraph that exemplify the characteristics of each category?
5. Are the categories distinct?

WRITING ASSIGNMENT 2

Classifying a Familiar Topic

Getting Ideas

BRAINSTORMING

For Writing Assignment 2, you will classify a topic of your choice that interests you. To begin, brainstorm a number of topics with your class. Choose topics that can be classified into categories.

As your instructor writes ideas on the board, choose one or two topics as a class and explore several ways of classifying each topic. For example, you might classify cars according to their types of designs, according to the ages of their owners, or according to the main ways their owners use them.

Here are some topic ideas:

love	cars	restaurants	holidays
marriage	housing	computers	transportation
books	friends	jobs	music
lies	excuses	study habits	husbands/wives
pets	sports	animals	dates

As you brainstorm, you may find it useful to narrow a broad topic. For example, if you choose the topic *holidays*, it may be easier to narrow the topic to holidays in your country.

OUTLINING
Use the guidelines on pages 179-180 to prepare an outline for this essay. Have your teacher or a classmate check the outline.

READING
Read this essay and discuss the questions that follow it with your class.

American Comedy Series

Since I came to the United States, I have enjoyed watching American comedy series on TV. At first, I didn't understand the differences between them. I only realized that some of these shows were boring while others weren't. I started to wonder what made these shows different. I soon found out that the main difference is the purpose of the comedies. In brief, American comedy series can be grouped into three categories, according to their intention: those that present indirect social messages, those that offer only fun, and those that show both characteristics just mentioned.

The first group of comedy series includes those that have indirect social messages. Their main purpose is to show a social situation through a story. They want the viewers to see situations like racial discrimination in a joking environment. Samples of this kind of show are *The Wonder Years, Where I Live,* and *Taxi.* The first one relates a man's story from his childhood to his adulthood. The second example presents the life of a young black man in a real New York neighborhood. Finally, *Taxi* is very interesting because it makes the viewers understand a little bit about the job and life of American taxi drivers. All these programs present their messages indirectly hidden in a comic story.

In contrast to the comedy shows with social messages, there are many funny shows in which the main intention is only fun. They are unbelievable; the actors do whatever they can to make the performance funny; no matter whether it is real or not, they do it. To find comedy series like these is easy since they exist in the greatest number. *The Small Wonder, The Monster Family,* and *Dinosaurs,* are clear representatives of these shows. In the first example, the main character is a simple and common girl with a weird voice and qualities of a robot. Even more unbelievable are *The Monster Family* and *Dinosaurs,* in which unreal monsters and creatures behave like human beings. This is exactly what makes them funny.

Finally, the last group of comedy series has not only indirect messages but also fun. The creators of this kind of comedy mix all the features of the other two categories; however, they don't care whether people catch the message or not. They are very popular, especially with adults and teenagers. *Murphy Brown* is an example of this kind of comedy show. In it, the job of the newscasters is less important than joking. Likewise, we find the same intention in comedies such as *Home Improvement* and *Full House.*

In conclusion, one of the reasons all the American comedy series are not the same is that each comedy has a different intention. We may infer that there are three groups of comedy shows according to their purposes: one that wants the viewers to catch the messages, another that only wants to focus on fun, and the last one, which combines both features.

Salem Waldron
Costa Rica

● **Discussion Questions:**

1. What is the thesis statement in the essay?

2. What is the principle of classification?

3. Unlike in the essay "Our Class's Relationship to Teachers," the thesis statement in this essay contains the categories. What are the categories?

4. How did the writer narrow his topic?

5. Which category is the least clear to you? Why? How could it be improved?

Writing

Write your classification essay. Make sure that you have a single principle of classification, well-defined categories and supporting examples.

Building Language Skillls

PARALLEL STRUCTURE

Here is a thesis statement introduced in Writing Assignment 1:

Students in my class can be classified according to the way they dress.

Now look at these two thesis statements:

Children's programs on television can be classified according to their purpose: those which primarily entertain, those which primarily educate, and those which attempt to both educate and entertain.

There are basically three types of TV news programs: local-news shows, national-news shows, and international-news shows.

These thesis statements are different from the ones introduced for Writing Assignment 1 in that in these the categories are included.

In introducing the three categories, the writers use parallel structure. Parallel structure means using identical grammatical forms. You need to use parallelism to list items in a series. The first thesis contains a series of adjective clauses; the second thesis has three nouns.

Here are some more sentences with parallel forms:

The students in my class are lazy, moderately hard-working, and studious. (series of adjectives)

He works energetically and diligently. (two adverbs)

She walked into the room and sat down. (two verbs)

Exercise 9.9   In the following sentences, underline the parallel items and identify their forms.

> *Example*   **He is a creative and humorous teacher. (adjectives)**

1. He is trying to lose weight and to stop smoking.

2. The buses are uncomfortable, dirty, and noisy.

3. The police provide the community with protection and security.

4. I prefer clothes that are casual but that look elegant.

5. My father answers my questions patiently and honestly.

6. In spite of the cold and rain, we did not cancel the trip.

7. We complained to the manager of the restaurant because the service was bad and the food wasn't fresh.

Exercise 9.10   In the following sentences, underline the item in the series that is *not* parallel, and correct it.

> *Example*   **She likes to get up early and jogging.**
>
> *She likes to get up early and jog.*

1. In choosing a place to live, a person may live in rural areas, in urban areas, and the suburbs.

2. Bicycles can be classified according to their purpose: those that are for racing, those that are for touring, and for mountain climbing.

3. I like to walk, to swim, and sunbathing at the beach.

4. Because of his patience and intelligent, I admire my teacher.

5. He has already passed the TOEFL test and enroll in the university.

Exercise 9.11   Complete the following sentences with parallel items.

> *Example*   **A person who is sincere and who respects others makes a good friend.**

1. American teens prefer to live alone and _____.

2. Computers have made our lives easier and _____.

3. He enjoys playing the guitar, _____, and _____.

4. She walked across the street and _____.

5. He wasn't accepted at the university because his grades were low and _____

_____.

6. A car should be dependable, _____, and _____.

7. The most important things in life are health, _____, and

_____.

VOCABULARY: INTENSIFIERS

When you name categories in classification writing, it's sometimes useful to have adverbs that can show you the intensity, or degree, of something.

For example, look at this sentence:

> **My homework can be classified as extremely challenging, somewhat challenging, or very easy.**

The adverbs *extremely, somewhat* and *very* help to differentiate the categories. These are adverbs that modify adjectives. They tell how intense the characteristic is.

Here is a list of useful intensifiers:

High	Medium	Low
extremely	somewhat	not very
very	moderately	slightly
incredibly	fairly	
	quite	

Revising

Share your classification essay with a partner and review each other's essays, using the points in the Writing Checklist. Revise your paper accordingly.

Writing Checklist

1. Does the essay use a single principle of classification?
2. Does the thesis statement introduce the classification and categories with parallel structures?
3. Does the essay contain well-defined categories?
4. Are the categories well supported by examples?

Journal Writing

A. Write a one-page entry in your journal on one of the following topics:

   1. What kind of animal would you like to be? Tell why.

   2. Compare yourself to a car. What kind of car are you like? Why?

B. Write one page in your journal on a topic of your choice.

More Writing Topics

1. Classify your friends.

2. Classify homework.

3. Classify the music that you like.

Chapter 10

The Global Community

What is one interesting thing that you have discovered about Americans since you came here?

What is one interesting thing you have learned about the culture of a classmate?

What is one difference you see in your culture and a particular classmate's culture?

Cultural Experiences

Getting Ideas

READING

Read the essay below, which was written as part of a student's application to attend a university. The student tells of a cultural lesson she learned while living and studying in the United States. This essay enabled the student to enroll in a prestigious private university; she had entered the U.S.A. at the age of 10, unable to speak English. When you have finished reading the essay, discuss the questions that follow with your class.

The Knowledge of Experience

Nowadays, a student's academic record plays a major role in his or her college acceptance. I feel that a good academic record should not be the only deciding factor. A student who does extremely well in learning only from books may not be successful in the real world. Knowledge is not only learned through books but is also obtained through experience and observation.

I was born in the People's Republic of China in 1975. I grew up in a completely different environment from the one I am living in now. To a child of ten, the enormous difference between China and the U.S.A. was not too great, except for the fact that I could not understand what everyone was saying. As I grew older, I began to notice the vast difference between two contrasting cultures. Every day, I feel the conflict between the Chinese and American cultures in my life. From five o'clock in the afternoon to seven in the morning, Chinese is my official language. I am surrounded by Chinese arts and music. But for the rest of the day, I become part of the American society. With such a schedule, the two nonuniform cultures cannot be severed completely. During the period when I am at home, I will get phone calls from English-speaking friends. Almost everything on television is in English as well. At school, I have many Chinese friends. Sometimes we will mention issues concerning China where Chinese has to be used to explain a point. There is hardly any time when the two cultures can be completely separated. I live in a world of two divergent cultures, but the American society has many dissimilar cultures tossed together.

Ever since I began taking courses in social science, I have learned that the American society is a gigantic "salad bowl." In the beginning of my middle-school years, this expression was just another locution I had to memorize for the upcoming history exam. I did not understand the entire meaning of the "salad bowl" until one of my most memorable experiences. I took dancing lessons from the sixth grade until the ninth grade. These lessons included ballet lessons as well as Chinese folk dances. Every year my dancing school would perform in the Houston International Festival. It was there that I gained my full understanding of the "salad bowl." I saw tents filled with souvenirs from countries all over the world. There were calligraphy writings from China, wooden sandals from Japan, blue porcelain decorative plates from the Netherlands, and much much more. People walked from tent to tent gazing at the many souvenirs, tasting the different types of food, and experiencing the various cultures from around the globe. Diverse cultures all merged together for a few days beneath the skyscrapers in downtown Houston before everything returned to normal everyday life. But for those few days, Houston was a "salad bowl" of mixed cultures.

After this rewarding experience, I began to take more notice of my surroundings. In Houston, there is hardly any major street that does not have at least one foreign restaurant or shop. There are also many ethnic restaurants where the food they serve has taken on American styles. One Chinese restaurant I visited served fried shrimp with the typical Chinese sweet and sour sauce. Chinese chefs usually do not fry anything except egg rolls. Due to the Americans' love for fried food, the chefs created their own culinary style of cooking, in which both Chinese and American tastes were satisfied.

A history book may be able to describe the "salad bowl" very well, but reading a book is completely different from experiencing it yourself. After my experience at the Houston International Festival and my many observations, I find that the phrase "salad bowl" is most appropriate for the American society. The diverse cultures are like the different ingredients which have been mixed in a bowl to make a salad. Indeed, books are good sources of basic knowledge, but once that knowledge has been learned, a better understanding of the knowledge can be obtained through real experiences and observations. This is the wisdom I have gained in my life. I value my excellent academic records as well as experiences. I will further improve my education and gain more experiences in my academic future.

"The knowledge of the world is only to be acquired in the world, and not in a closet."
—Lord Chesterfield

Yiyang Jenny Wang
U.S.A.

Discussion:

1. What is the thesis of this essay?

2. What is the main idea of body paragraph 1?

3. In body paragraph 1, Wang writes, "I live in a world of two divergent cultures, but the American society has many dissimilar cultures tossed together." What does she mean?

4. In body paragraph 2, what is the main idea?

5. What experience made her truly understand the sentence, "The American society is a gigantic 'salad bowl.'"?

6. After this experience, what else did she notice to reinforce the notion of the "salad bowl"?

7. Have you noticed any mixing of cultures in the U.S.? Think of some examples.

8. In her essay, Wang says she realizes that knowledge is gained through experience and observation. Using your experience and observations, discuss what have you learned about American culture or the different cultures represented in your class.

FREEWRITING

Yiyang Jenny Wang wrote about one experience that taught her something about American culture. The meaningful lesson that she learned was that knowledge comes from experience, not just from books. In her life, her experiences have been multicultural.

You have also experienced the impact of different cultures. Think about one thing you have learned about a culture other than your own—perhaps American culture or a classmate's culture.

The thing you have learned may have to do with day-to-day experiences—like food, conversational styles, women's and men's roles, dating styles, or classroom etiquette, for example. Think of one aspect of a different culture that you have learned about.

Write for five minutes about one thing you have learned about a different culture.

BRAINSTORMING

When you have finished, share your paper with a small group. Discuss what each of you wrote about, and compare your experiences.

As you discuss cultural topics, think about other things you have learned about American culture or about other cultures in your class.

Use these lines to make notes about three or four things you have learned:

1. _____

2. _____

3. _____

4. _____

Composing

THESIS STATEMENT

Your writing assignment will be to write about what you have discovered about American culture or what you have learned about other cultures in your class.

When you have chosen two or three cultural topics to write about, you will be ready to prepare a thesis statement. Your two or three ideas should be introduced in the thesis statement.

Look at these sample thesis statements:

> **I have learned several things about the cultures of the international students in my classes since I have been a student in the United States.**

> **During my stay in the United States, I have learned that Americans like to drive fast and to eat fast.**

The first sentence indicates that in her essay the writer will present three things that she has learned about the different cultures in her class. She does not specify the three things in her thesis statement.

In the second thesis, the writer will present two facts she has learned about American culture: that Americans like to drive fast and that they like to eat fast. In this thesis statement, the two items in the group are expressed with parallel grammatical structures.

Exercise 10.1 Write your thesis statement here:

_____

_____

If you have specified the two or three cultural facts that you have learned, check with your instructor to see that you expressed each fact in a parallel form.

Getting Ideas

READING

The essay below, "Things That Affected Me When I Came to the United States," deals with three difficulties that a student faced in her new culture. With your classmates, answer the questions that follow after you read.

Things That Affected Me When I Came to the United States

It doesn't matter to which country you go. You are always going to find some things different from things in your country of origin. When I came to the United States, three things affected me.

The first thing that affected me was the language. My native language is Spanish, so I didn't know how to speak English and I had to learn it. I knew a little English but just the basics, and I needed to practice a lot. Because I wasn't able to speak English fluently, I felt inferior to the people that were around me. As a result, I got depressed frequently. My personality changed from talkative to quiet. Each time that my husband and I went to a party where the people spoke only English, I just listened to what the people said, and I never gave my opinion on the subject that they were talking about because I thought that I wouldn't be able to explain my thoughts. Many times I imagined myself making the sentence in English of what I wanted to say. If it sounded good, I said it, but if it did not, I just looked at everyone talking, hoping that someone said what I was thinking. I felt like a child.

Another thing that affected me when I came to the United States was the cold relationship among people. In Mexico, my country of origin, the people are warm. If they don't know you, they might say, "hello" to introduce themselves and to start a conversation. Different from my compatriots, however, Americans are very emotionless. In general, U.S. citizens don't care if they talk to you or not. They live their own lives, and whether you are their friend or not is irrelevant. The most I can get from American people is a smile. This month I will celebrate my first year living in my townhouse, and I don't know my neighbors. On the left side of the house lives a girl named Angie, whom I just talked to about plants once in April. On the other side lives a couple with a little girl, whom I have never talked to. I don't know what my neighbors do for a living, where they are from, or what they like to do in their free time. This coldness made me feel lonely when I was alone during the days before I started school.

Finally, the last thing that has affected me since I came to the United States is my professional status. When I decided to come to the United States, I didn't realize that I was throwing my journalism career in the trash can. There are several reasons why it is difficult for me to find a job in my profession. First, my career depends on writing, which means I have to dominate the English language. Second, there are only a few TV stations where I can work in Houston. And finally, my degree is not valid here. I feel that I lost four years of studying since a lot of my classes are not accepted for credit here. Also, I don't have previous employment experience in the United States, and it is very important to have a work record. I have to start working in grocery stores or in a mall while I study a different major. This is very frustrating.

In conclusion, when I came to the United States, three things affected me: the English language, coldness of American people, and my professional status. The first one I have overcome. For the second one, I just have to find the right warm people and get used to the remainder. The third one just depends on me. I hope that in the near future I will be working in a field that I like.

Palmira Yvette Ramirez
Mexico

Discussion:

1. What is the thesis statement?

2. What is the topic sentence of body paragraph 1?

3. What support is used in this paragraph for the topic sentence?

4. What is the topic sentence of body paragraph 2? paragraph 3?

5. What support is used in these paragraphs for the topic sentences?

6. Besides restating the thesis statement, how does the writer conclude her essay?

7. Do you share any of the feelings that this student has?

Composing

OUTLINING

When you have written a thesis statement, you can prepare an outline for your assignment. Use this suggested plan:

I. Introduction
    Thesis statement: Identify what you have learned about American culture.
    or
    Identify what you have learned about another culture of one of your classmates.

    Example thesis statement: **I have discovered several cultural facts about Americans during my stay in the United States.**

II. Body Paragraph 1: Introduce the first cultural observation you have learned.

    Example topic sentence: **First, Americans eat too much.**

    Support: Use at least two examples, details, or other supporting ideas to illustrate the cultural fact.

III. Body paragraph 2: Introduce the second cultural observation you have learned.

    Example topic sentence: **Besides overeating, Americans also love shopping.**

    Support: Use at least two examples, details, or other supporting ideas to illustrate the cultural fact.

IV. Body paragraph 3: Introduce the third cultural observation you have learned.

    Example topic sentence: **Finally, Americans spoil their children.**

    Support: Use at least two examples, details, or other supporting ideas to illustrate the cultural fact.

V. Conclusion: Restate the thesis statement. Comment on the cultural facts that you have written about.

Writing

After you have an outline, write your essay about what you have learned about a culture that is different from your own. For the benefit of your audience, identify both your native culture and the different culture by name. Explain the differences so that a reader from yet another culture can understand your perspective.

Consider these points on the Writing Checklist before you write.

Writing Checklist

1. Does your thesis statement present what you have learned about the culture, either specifically or generally?
2. Do each of the topic sentences tell about one cultural observation?
3. Are there at least two pieces of supporting information in each body paragraph?
4. Does the conclusion comment about the cultural observations?
5. Have you paid careful attention to the shift of verb tenses in your writing?

Building Language Skills

PRESENT PERFECT TENSE

Look at these thesis statements, which were first presented on page 195. Both use the present perfect tense, which you studied in chapter 7.

> **During my stay in the United States, I have learned that Americans like to drive fast and to eat fast.**

> **I have learned several things about the cultures of the international students in my classes since I have been a student in the United States.**

In each sentence, at what time does the learning take place?

The present perfect tense not only describes past to present time. It may also be used to write about actions that have happened in the past, but not at a definite time; look at this sentence, for example:

> **I have discovered many truths about Americans.**

For this assignment, you may use the present perfect to describe cultural facts that you have learned over a period of time up to the present or at an indefinite time in the past.

Exercise 10.2   Read the sentences below in which the present perfect should be used, and correct the sentences.

1. I live in the United States for six months.

2. Over the past year, I learned many things about different cultures.

3. Since I came to this country, I met many people from across the world.

4. I saw several cultural differences between myself and my classmates since I arrived in the U.S.

5. I change my ideas about Chinese people.

6. Time passed, and I have discovered many new aspects of this culture.

SHIFTING VERB TENSE

For this assignment, you will probably use a variety of verb tenses in the introduction and conclusion to discuss what you "know," what you "have learned," or what you "will remember" about your cultural experiences.

When you tell the stories of these specific experiences, you will probably use past tense verbs such as *met, was studying,* or *had never known.*

Try to separate in your mind the various "times" you are in as you write. Remember to rely most on the simple past tense to tell a past story, and use other past-time verbs as necessary. Shift to other verb tenses as you explain how you "feel" now, what you "have realized," or how these experiences "will affect" you.

Exercise 10.3   Complete the passage below with the appropriate verbs. Keep in the mind the "time" of each part of the writing.

Today is June 13. My car _____ (be) in the shop for three weeks, so this morning I

_____ (call) the repairman and _____ (say) that I _____

(want) them to finish my car before next Tuesday or I _____ (take) my money back.

I _____ (have) this car for three months. During this time, I _____ (call)

someone to tow my car four times. I _____ (be) really tired of this terrible car. Before

I _____ (buy) it, I _____ (think) buying a car would save me time. But

now, it only _____ (make) more trouble for me. I _____ (change) all the

parts but the motor. I _____ (promise) that if someday I _____ (not

need) a car anymore, I _____ (burn) it and _____ (push) it into a river.

Ming-Lun Lee
Taiwan

VOCABULARY: WRITING ABOUT CULTURAL DISCOVERIES

Look at these sentences:

I have learned many interesting things about American culture.

Some parts of American culture are shocking.

Focus on three words in the sentences that are often overused in English:

learned   **things**   **parts**

Can you think of other ways to express each idea?

Here is one possible revision:

> **I have <u>observed</u> many interesting <u>details</u> about American culture.**
>
> **Some <u>aspects</u> of American culture are shocking**

This sentence contains three words that you might not immediately choose to express the ideas of "learn," "things," and "parts." The writer was looking for a new way to state his thoughts, so he consulted *Webster's New Dictionary of Synonyms.*

You can also use *Roget's Thesaurus* or another synonym-antonym book, as you have learned in earlier chapters, to help you select appropriate synonymous phrases. Use a dictionary or one of those synonym books to find new ways to state your ideas.

A. To Learn

Learn is one of the first verbs that you meet in English. It's an all-purpose word that fits many situations, but there are also many other ways to express this idea.

Write another verb that means *learned* in this sentence:

> **One fact that I have <u>learned</u> about many Koreans is that they are very friendly.**
>
> *Example*   _____

Here are a few suggestions:

discovered   determined   ascertained   uncovered   unearthed

B. Things

The words *thing* and *something* are often overused. *Thing* is such a general word in English that it can relate an object, an event, an abstract feeling, or a detail.

For this writing assignment, explore other ways to express the "things" that you have learned about different cultures.

Begin by thinking of a substitute word or phrase to complete this sentence:

> **One <u>thing</u> I have learned about Japanese culture is that Japanese people love to <u>joke</u>.**
>
> *Example*   _____

You could use words like these in the sentence above:

truth	**lesson**	**fact**	**piece of knowledge**
detail	**piece of information (non-count)**		

C. Parts

You may also want to write about a "part" of a culture about which you have learned a fact.

Think of substitute words for *part* in this sentence:

> **One <u>part</u> of Chinese culture that I have investigated is the Chinese language, which <u>has</u> many different tones.**

Example   _____   _____

Here are some other words you might use to express the idea of "part":

aspect   **area**   **realm**   **facet**   **side**

Exercise 10.4   Look again at the essay "Things That Affected Me When I Came to the United States" on pages 195–196. In the introduction and for each topic sentence in the body paragraphs, choose other words to replace the word *thing*, or any word which the author overuses.

Exercise 10.5   Write three sentences in which you describe "things" you have "learned" about "parts" of a different culture. Try to use new words.

Example   **I have *uncovered* a great deal of *new information* about certain *facets* of Japanese culture.**

Revising

Have a partner read your essay about what you have learned about a culture different from your own. Then, ask your partner to evaluate it on the basis of the Writing Checklist questions on page 198. Also, ask your partner to consider these additional questions:

1. Is the paper interesting?

2. Are the cultural facts presented in a clear way?

3. Has the writer convinced you that his or her opinions are logical?

4. Do verb tenses appropriately reflect the various "times" in the writing?

5. Does the writer overuse words in the essay? Could you suggest synonyms for some of these words?

A Campus Survey

Getting Ideas

BRAINSTORMING

One way to gain a sense of American culture is to conduct a survey on a controversial subject. This not only gives you an insight into this society's cultural values, but it also tells you something about your own culture.

To conduct a survey of American students, begin by thinking of an educational, social, or global issue that you think young people will have strong views about. Choose a topic for which there is ample support on two sides—in other words, a topic that will evoke a variety of responses and opinions.

You will choose your own survey topic. Begin by thinking of general subject areas for the survey. You can formulate the actual survey question later.

Here are a few ideas for survey topics:

the ideal mate	the meaning of success
homeless people	film/TV censorship
abortion	being single or married
handgun ownership	premarital cohabitation
foreign-student tuition	reason for getting a college degree
the future of families	how to save money
top jobs of the future	favorite college class

With a small group, brainstorm a general topic for your survey. You may use one of the topics suggested here, or think of a different topic. To get ideas, you might first think of a broad subject area like *education,* and then focus on one controversial aspect of the topic, such as *the cost of a college education.*

As you write down subject ideas, try to select a subject that will interest you and your class as well as the students who will respond to your survey questions. Also, choose a subject that students are aware of. For example, a subject like childcare will only interest students who have children. Also, a subject such as taxation is one that some students will have little information about.

Considering these suggestions, decide on two or three subject ideas, and share them with the rest of the class. Ask your classmates to help you evaluate them.

FORMULATING A SURVEY QUESTION

When your group has generated a few good survey subjects, you and one partner from your group will write a survey question which you two will ask together.

Keep the following recommendations in mind when you write the question.

1. You need to be able to easily organize your survey results. Therefore, include a word in your question that suggests a way to organize the responses into an essay format. You might use words such as these in your question:

   way(s)/method(s)

   cause(s)/reason(s)

   effect(s)/benefit(s)/disadvantage(s)

   type(s)/kind(s)

   quality(ies)/characteristic(s)

   Example question: **In what ways should the government control TV content?**

Using the word *ways* in this question will allow you to organize the essay into body paragraphs, each of which will discuss one "way" to control TV content.

2. Another way to phrase your question so that the responses are easily organized into an essay is to ask a *yes-no* question. However, you should always follow it with another question, such as *why*, or *why or why not?*

   Example question: **Should a couple live together before marriage? Why or why not?**

3. Remember to write a question that you think the student respondents will have mixed views about. For instance, if you ask, "Should the U.S. government help homeless people?" most respondents will answer "yes." This question will not give you interesting results. However, you might get more varied responses if you use one of the words in suggestion number 1: "In what ways should the U.S. government help homeless people?"

4. Keep your question simple. That will make it easier for respondents to answer and for you to record the answers.

Have you and your partner come up with a tentative survey question? Write it here:

_____

READING

Read the following essay, which is based on the survey question, "What are the benefits of working while attending college?" Then, discuss the questions that follow with your classmates.

The Benefits of Working

Nowadays many college students work out of necessity. All students need money to pay for tuition and books as well as other living costs. For many, the only way to do this is to work. In a recent survey, twenty-five American students at the University of Houston-Downtown said that although working is difficult, it has several advantages.

Of course, the main benefit that students get from working while going to school is financial support. Many students said that they could not afford to attend college if they did not work, even though most of them received financial assistance from their families. Sandra Webb, a junior in mathematics, said, "Working and studying is really hard, but I couldn't stay in school if I didn't work." Mike Matthews, a senior and an English major, agreed. He said that his parents paid for his first year of college but that they weren't able to help him after that. He explained, "I started working full-time and going to school at night. It's been a lot slower this way, but at least I'm still in school."

Another important advantage of working is gaining work experience. Most students said that they had learned important job skills while they worked. Some students said they had gotten positions that would help them in their career. John Askins, a freshman majoring in business, works at Mr. Gatti's Pizza in the evenings and on weekends. He said the work is not prestigious, but it will give him some job experience and a reference for his résumé. Askins added, "I've learned a lot about how a food business operates." Eric Connors, a junior in computer science, said his job as a student assistant in the university's computing lab brought him a great deal of practical knowledge about computer software and hardware. Connors stated, "Every day I find out something new. This job will give me a definite plus when I finish school and start job hunting."

Finally, many students reported that they think their work has helped them learn other adult skills. Jessica McKay, a senior who is majoring in applied engineering, said she worked at Randall's as a cashier during her first year of college. McKay said, "This was the first job I had ever had. I was pretty naive about how to get along with people and how to be responsible. I mean, you have to handle a lot of money, and if you make a mistake, you have to pay. That taught me a lot." McKay added that her later jobs, as a waitress and as a department-store clerk, taught her responsibility. Tanya Roberts, a sophomore in computer science, said her job as a cashier at the university bookstore has helped her manage her money better. She said, "When I first started working, I didn't know how to stay in a budget. I couldn't even balance my checkbook! Now, I watch what I spend, and I'm even more serious about my studies, because I know I'm working to help pay for them."

For all the students, working and going to college at the same time was difficult. But they said the pluses outweighed the minuses. In my opinion, it would be better if students didn't have to work. Then, they could concentrate on their studying. However, if a student has to work, he or she should try to work only part-time. When I begin academic classes, I may have to get a job, but I hope that it will have some benefits for me, too.

Discussion:

1. What is the topic of the essay? Is this subject interesting?

2. What is the thesis statement?

3. Does the thesis specify the survey group? the survey results?

4. What are the three logical groups into which the survey responses were divided? Which sentences identify these groups?

5. What kind of support is used in each body paragraph?

6. How did the survey question make organizing the essay easier?

7. Does the interviewer give her opinion? If so, where?

Getting Ideas

CONDUCTING THE SURVEY

When you and your partner have agreed on a survey question, check your question with your instructor to see if it is grammatically correct and if it will generate responses that can be organized into an essay.

Now, you and your partner will share the responsibility of conducting survey interviews and recording the responses. You will probably need to conduct between fifteen and twenty-five interviews to get ample results. Your instructor will assign the exact number for you to do.

Follow these guidelines when you interview:

- Take turns. Both you and your partner should ask the question during interviews.

- Rehearse. With your partner, practice what you will say as you approach a potential respondent. Also, practice identifying yourselves and the reasons for your survey (for example, a class assignment or your interest in learning about American culture). Ask your instructor for a few suggestions on how to "break the ice." Generally, if you are polite, you should have no trouble getting responses.

- Record and take notes. To record the interviews, use a dual system of note taking and recording the conversation on a tape recorder, if possible. One of you can take notes while the other listens and talks to the interviewee, or both you and your partner can take notes. Always ask the interviewee if you can record his or her response before you begin taping.

- Get names and in addition to the response, get the student's full name and classification and major. Ask the student to spell his or her name. *Classification* refers to the year of study at a university; *major* means the field of study. Ask for permission to use your respondent's name in a class essay.

● **Exercise 10.6** In front of your class, conduct a practice interview with your partner. Have classmates evaluate your interview.

Composing

ORGANIZING THE RESULTS

Now that you have gathered a set amount of survey responses, your task will be to "translate" each interview into a brief, legible form (either on a computer or a typewriter, or in legible handwriting).

With your partner, review the audiotaped recording of each interview. Match the recording with your notes. If you both have taken notes, compare these to compile a complete but succinct record of each conversation.

When you have finished, make a legible copy of your notes for yourself and your partner.

To organize your responses for your essays, you and your partner will work separately. Each of you must examine the responses and group them into logical categories. For example, imagine that you have asked this question:

Should the university cut its tuition in half?

You might have fifteen respondents who answered affirmatively, five who answered negatively, and another five who answered "in the middle." You could group those responses into these three categories.

Another possible survey question might be this one:

What quality is most important to you in a romantic partner?

Here, you may have a range of answers, but you will need to organize them in a logical way. Perhaps you have five respondents who said "beauty" was the most important characteristic; six who answered, "intelligence"; five who said "honesty" was the most important quality;

and four more who gave four different responses. One way to group these responses might be to throw out the four different responses; another way might be to characterize the last group as miscellaneous responses and to use the other three groups as categories.

Look over your survey results and put the responses into three or four logical groups.

_____

_____

_____

_____

WRITING A THESIS STATEMENT

In this essay, you will be reporting the opinions of a group of American students. Your purpose is to gain an insight into this culture. Therefore, your main idea sentence should contain certain information:

- It should identify the subject of the survey.
- It should identify the group you have surveyed.
- It should introduce the logical groups of the response.

Compare these examples of acceptable thesis statements for an essay reporting survey results:

> **Most students interviewed at Georgetown University said that beauty, intelligence. and honesty are the most important qualities in a mate.**

> **In a recent survey, a majority of the students interviewed at the University of Houston-Downtown gave several reasons why the university should not require students to pass the Junior Proficiency Exam.**

Both of the above thesis statements are acceptable ways to express the main idea of the essay. The first thesis statement is more specific because it states the three qualities: "beauty, intelligence, and honesty." The second thesis is more general because it does not directly state the "reasons" the students gave in the survey about the Junior Proficiency Exam.

Here are some useful expressions for a thesis statement about survey results:

| **In a recent survey,** | **According to** |
| **A recent survey shows/indicates** | **In the opinion of** |

Exercise 10.7   Using the information that follows, write a possible thesis statement for an essay which reports the results of a survey. In these thesis statements, you will give specific information about the group being surveyed.

Example	Respondents:	**American students at the University of Pennsylvania**
	Survey question:	**Should abortion be legal or illegal in the United States? Why?**
	Responses:	**Most students said abortion should be legal for three main reasons.**

Possible Thesis Statement:

Most students at the University of Pennsylvania believe that abortion should be legal for three main reasons, according to a recent survey.

1. Respondents: American students at Loyola University
   Survey question: Should the tuition for foreign students be the same as the tuition for Americans?
   Responses: Foreign tuition should be higher for three main reasons.
   Possible Thesis Statement:

   _____

   _____

2. Respondents: American students at Wayne State University
   Survey question: Should the U.S. government strictly limit immigration?
   Responses: The U.S. government should not strictly limit immigration for three important reasons.
   Possible thesis statement:

   _____

   _____

3. Respondents: American students at Community College of Philadelphia
   Survey question: What do you think will be the top jobs of the future?
   Responses: In the future, the best jobs will be in computer science, medicine, and business.
   Possible thesis statement:

   _____

   _____

THESIS STATEMENT/OUTLINING

Write your thesis statement here:

_____

_____

After you have a thesis statement and topic sentences in mind, you can prepare an outline for your essay. Here is a suggested way to organize your results.

I.   Introduction
   Thesis Statement: Introduce the survey topic, identify the respondents, and state the survey results.

Example thesis statement: **In a recent survey, American students at Houston Community College said the government should prohibit the ownership of handguns for three main reasons.**

II.   Body paragraph 1: Introduce the first logical group.

Example topic sentence: **One reason handgun ownership should be banned is that handguns are involved in many accidental deaths.**

Support: Summarize what students said about this point. Use direct speech or reported speech to tell about at least two of the responses. (See pages 212–215.)

III. Body paragraph 2: Introduce the second logical group.

Example topic sentence: **Besides accidental deaths, handguns also figure in many crime-related deaths.**

Support: Summarize what students said about this point. Use direct speech or reported speech to tell about at least two of the responses.

IV.   Body paragraph 3: Introduce the third logical group.

Example topic sentence: **Most important, handguns are used in deaths that occur among friends and family.**

Support: Summarize what students said about this point. Use direct speech or reported speech to tell about at least two of the responses.

V.   Conclusion: Restate the thesis statement. Give your opinion about the survey question or an explanation of what people said: What is your opinion on the question? If you disagree with the opinion in the survey results, what is your reaction to that opinion?

Writing

Use the information you have gained from your survey, the outline, and the reading to help you organize and write an essay about your survey question.

Before you write, consider the Writing Checklist questions below:

```
╔══════════════════════════════════════════════════════════════╗
                    Writing Checklist

    1. Does your thesis statement introduce the survey question, identify the
       respondents, and state the survey results?
    2. Are the results organized into three or four logical groups?
    3. Does each body paragraph contain a topic sentence and support that
       relate to each logical group?
    4. Does the conclusion summarize the respondents' opinions and give the
       writer's opinion on the question?
╚══════════════════════════════════════════════════════════════╝
```

Building Language Skills

FORMING QUESTIONS

Before you embark on your survey, check your question for grammatical accuracy. Remember that a question follows this word order:

Auxiliary Verb + Subject + (Main Verb) + Rest of Sentence

or

Wh-Word + Auxiliary Verb + Subject + (Main Verb) + Rest of Sentence

Here are a few model questions:

Is it better to be rich and unhappy or to be poor and happy?

What are the advantages or disadvantages of having sex education in public schools?

What is the best way to achieve long life?

Do AIDS sufferers have a right to free health care?

Look at the last sentence. Why is the *do* auxiliary used? When do you use *do* in questions?

Exercise 10.8   Check the grammatical accuracy of these questions. Some contain errors; others are correct. Edit the errors above each line.

1. How you can save money?

2. What is means success?

3. What characteristics an ideal mate has?

4. Should foreign-student tuition higher than resident tuition?

5. Is a college education valuable? Why or why not?

PARALLEL STRUCTURE

Look again at this thesis statement for an essay reporting survey results:

> **Most students interviewed at Georgetown University said that beauty, intelligence, and honesty are the most important qualities in a mate.**

What are the three qualities that the writer expresses? In what form is each quality expressed (that is, as a *noun, verb, adjective,* or *adverb*)?

In the thesis statement above, the three qualities are expressed in parallel noun forms. If you write a similar thesis, be sure to list each of the logical groups, such as qualities/ways/types/effects/causes, in parallel form.

Exercise 10.9 Write thesis statements, using the information that follows. Be sure that each of the logical groups is expressed with parallel structures.

Example
Respondents: American students at Indiana State University
Survey question: Should student and staff parking be free?
Why or why not?
Results: Most students said student and staff parking should be free for three reasons.
1. High cost of student tuition and fees
2. The staff work for the university
3. Parking is free at a nearby university.
Possible thesis statement:
Most students polled at Indiana State University said that student and staff parking should be free because the students pay high tuition and fees, because the staff work for the university, and because parking is free at a nearby university.

1. Respondents: American students at New York University
   Survey question: Should couples live together before marriage? Why or why not?
   Results: Most students said if couples live together before marriage they can learn many things about each other.

   • Bad habits

   • The depth of their love

   • Whether they share common interests

   Possible thesis statement:

   _____

   _____

2. Respondents: American students at San Francisco State University
   Survey question: Why are you attending the university?
   Results: Most students gave three reasons for attending the university.
   - Because they want to get a good job (money)
   - To gain a broad education
   - To learn specific skills for their jobs

   Possible thesis statement:

   _____

   _____

3. Respondents: American students at Arizona State University
   Survey question: What is the meaning of success?
   Results: Most students said "success" means three things to them.
   - Money
   - Having a family
   - To enjoy good health

   Possible thesis statement:

   _____

   _____

DIRECT SPEECH

Before you write your essay, consider how you will report the survey results in the body paragraphs. Look at this possible response:

> **Question:** **Should the university provide free health-care services to all of its students, faculty, and staff?**
>
> **Response:** **No, I don't think so. I think the university would end up spending a bundle of money on this. The school might have to close because it wouldn't have any money left.**

How can you incorporate this idea in the body of an essay?

One way is to use direct speech, that is, to quote exactly the words of the respondent.

> **John Doe, a freshman in biology, said, "I think the university would end up spending a bundle of money on this. The school might have to close because it wouldn't have any money left."**

Notice how the sentence is punctuated. A comma comes after *said*. Quotation marks open and close the response, and a period comes before the final quotation mark. The verb *said* introduces the respondent, who is identified by name, classification, and major. The name, classification, and major are set off by commas.

Read the body paragraph below, which contains a topic sentence, a summary of the reasons given for the opinion, and two direct-speech quotations as support:

The first reason that students gave for not offering free health care for students, faculty, and staff was the high cost. Students said the university would spend thousands of dollars a day if all the health care were free. John Doe, a freshman in biology, said, "I think the university would end up spending a bundle of money on this. The school might have to close because it wouldn't have any money left." Sarah Smith, a junior in accounting, agreed. "Imagine how much money this might cost the university," she said. "If 100 people visited the health center every day, it might cost the university $3,000 a day!" Most of the students said they believed the service would be very popular, and, thus, very expensive for the university.

Notice again the punctuation for the students' names, classifications, and majors, as well as for the quotations.

Exercise 10.10   Write sentences using direct speech.

Example   **I don't think international students should pay three times as much tuition as American students. That's ridiculous.**

—Stephen Bower, sophomore, computer science

Stephen Bower, a sophomore in computer science, said, "I don't think international students should pay three times as much tuition as American students. That's ridiculous."

1. Why shouldn't we have prayer in public schools? Aren't most people religious?

   —Joe Schmidt, freshman, undecided major

2. Maybe some people think TV is a waste of time, but I don't. It relaxes me, and it helps me unwind after a hard day.

   —Marsha Cantor, senior, English

3. How can you expect me to work and study? Give me a break.

   —Stacey Parker, sophomore, architecture

4. Yeah, how can you have any fun if you don't drink? I don't have a good time unless I go to a club and drink with my friends.

   —Ray Beisel, senior, electrical engineering

5. Marriage is every woman's fulfillment. I would feel like half a person if I never married.

   —Nancy Sloan, freshman, English

INDIRECT SPEECH

Another way to report what somone has said is through indirect speech.

Look at this response to the survey question, "Is it better to be married or single?"

I don't want to live alone, so marriage is better for me.

—Janet Myers, sophomore, chemistry

You can directly quote the student in your essay:

Janet Myers, a sophomore in chemistry, said, "I don't want to live alone, so marriage is better for me."

Or you can use indirect speech:

Janet Myers, a sophomore in chemistry, said she didn't want to live alone, so marriage was better for her.

The punctuation is different between the two sentences above, and you can also see a number of grammatical differences.

Look at the chart that follows to see how the verb tenses change when direct speech is changed to indirect speech.

Direct Speech	Indirect Speech
"I work."	John said that he worked.
"I am working."	John said that he was working.
"I worked."	John said that he had worked.
"I was working."	John said that he had been working.
"I have worked."	John said that he had worked.
"I have been working."	John said that he had been working.
"I had worked."	John said that he had worked.
"I will work."	John said that he would work.
"I can work."	John said that he could work.
"I may work."	John said that he might work.
"I have to work.	John said that he had to work.

Also, the pronouns must shift when direct speech is changed to indirect speech.

Examples   **John: "I want a rich wife."**
John said (that) he wanted a rich wife.   (present to past)

Rick: "I worked at McDonald's for two years."
Rick said (that) he had worked at McDonald's for two years.   (past to past perfect)

In indirect speech, the word *that* to introduce the statement may be omitted.

Indirect speech can also be used when you report a question.

Examples **Suzanne: "Does the perfect job exist?" (present to past)**
Suzanne wondered if the perfect job existed.

Tom: "Did the university always accept international students?"
(past to past perfect)
Tom asked whether the university had always accepted
international students.

Notice that the words *if* and *whether* are necessary to introduce the question.

Consult a grammar book for more detailed information about the structure of indirect speech.

Exercise 10.11 Change the direct speech reports that follow into indirect speech. For each sentence, identify the respondent as "one student" (male).

Example **"My favorite college course was an art history course that I took for fun."**

One student said (that) his favorite college course was an art history course (that) he had taken for fun.

1. "I want to give tents to all homeless people."

   _____

2. "The best way to save money is to spend less money."

   _____

3. "I think it's ridiculous that they censor TV in the United States."

   _____

4. "There's no easy way to lose weight, but I still keep trying."

   _____

5. "The main reason I want a college degree is so that I can get a good job."

   _____

VOCABULARY: VERBS TO INTRODUCE SPEECH STATEMENTS

To introduce what someone has said, you can use the verb *say* as well as many other verbs.

Look at this passage from the reading, "The Benefits of Working":

McKay said, "This was the first job I had ever had. I was pretty naive about how to get along with people and how to be responsible. I mean, you have to handle a lot of money, and if you make a mistake, you have to pay. That taught me a lot." McKay added that her later jobs, as a waitress and as a department-store clerk, also taught her responsibility.

Here, the writer uses *said* and *added* to introduce speech statements. Here, the verb *said* introduces the first statement by the interviewee, and the verb *added* introduces a second statement.

You can use a variety of verbs to introduce speech. Use verbs that suit the context of the spoken statement, as the writer does here. For example, verbs like *agreed* or *disagreed* can be used to introduce second statements, and verbs like *argued* or *contended* can introduce statements that indicate strong belief.

Here are some useful verbs to introduce speech statements:

Say (neutral)	Answer	Ask	Agree	Believe Strongly
say	answer	ask	agree	argue
tell (someone) (something)	respond	wonder	disagree	contend
report	retort	want to know		
state				
explain				
add				

Exercise 10.12   Find the verbs used to introduce speech statements in "The Benefits of Working." Discuss why each verb is used.

Exercise 10.13   Read the passage below. Substitute verbs for the word *said* where it is appropriate to do so.

Many students said another problem with attending night courses was that many university offices are closed after 5 P.M. Bud Shaw, a sophomore in mechanical engineering, said if he wanted to cash a check or buy a bus pass, he couldn't do it at night. "The university doesn't have any consideration for night students," he said. "I think if they (the university administrators) had to be here at night, these offices would be open." Shaw said he would rather not attend night classes, but he had to work during the day. "I haven't got any other choice," he said. Shaw said that he had been attending night classes for two semesters, while working as a mail sorter for a private mailing company.

Revising

Exchange papers with your survey partner. Evaluate each other's papers on the basis of the Writing Checklist questions on page 210. Revise your paper as necessary.

Journal Writing

A. Write a one-page entry in your journal on one of these topics:

1. Tell about when you first arrived in the United States and you made a cultural "mistake" by following your culture instead of American culture.

2. Write about one interesting person from another culture.

B. Write one page on a free topic of your choice.

More Writing Topics

1. Write about three stereotypes about people from your country.

2. Write about one stereotype that you had about people from a particular country that you later found was untrue. Tell how you got this idea originally and how you later learned it was false.

Credits

(Page numbers are given in boldface.)

PHOTOS

1: (top left) Peter Menzel; (top right) Rhoda Sidney, The Image Works; (bottom left) Michael McGovern, The Picture Cube; (bottom right) Sarah Putnam, The Picture Cube. **7:** Gary A. Conner, PhotoEdit. **23:** Robert E. Daemmrich, Tony Stone Worldwide/Chicago. **34:** James L. Shaffer, PhotoEdit. **45:** Michael Weisbrot, Stock, Boston. **57:** Nita Winter, The Image Works. **67:** Jean-Claude Lejeune, Stock, Boston. **68:** (left) Leland Bobbe, Tony Stone Worldwide; (right) Walter S. Silver, The Picture Cube. **69:** (left) Michael Weisbrot, Stock, Boston; (right) Jean-Claude Lejeune, Stock, Boston. **91:** Michael Dwyer, Stock, Boston. **103:** Gale Zucker, Stock, Boston. **111:** Kathy McLaughlin, The Image Works. **124:** Charles Osgood, Tony Stone Images. **129:** Kindra Clineff, The Picture Cube. **148:** Dion Ogust, The Image Works. **153:** (top) Tony Freeman, PhotoEdit; (bottom) Nissan North America, Inc. **170:** Rhoda Sidney, Stock, Boston. **173:** Joseph Schuyler, Stock, Boston. **187:** Fredrik Bodin, Stock, Boston. **191:** Phillip Hayson, Photo Researchers. **206:** E. Crews, The Image Works.

TEXT

3: Personal T-Shirts exercise from TRIBES, A Process for Social Development and Cooperative Learning, 1987 Jeanne Gibbs, Center Source Publications, Santa Rosa, CA 94501 (707)577-8233. **130:** "Man in the Mirror" (Siedah Garrett, Glen Ballard) © 1987 Yellow Brick Road Music & MCA Music Publishing, a Division of MCA, Inc. All rights on behalf of Yellow Brick Road Music, for the world, excluding Japan, Brazil and Hong Kong, administered by WB Music Corp. All Rights Reserved. Used by permission.